CAN I GIVE THEM BACK NOW?

CAN I GIVE THEM BACK NOW?

The Aargh to Zzzz of Parenting

Joanna Simmons and Jay Curtis

 SQUARE PEG

LONDON

Published by Square Peg

2 4 6 8 10 9 7 5 3 1

Copyright © Joanna Simmons and Jay Curtis 2009

Lyrics from Those Were The Days by Gene Raskin © 1968 & 1974 TRO Essex Music Inc, USA assigned to: TRO Essex Music LTD. International Copyright Secured. All rights reserved. by Permission.

Lyrics from by Chas Hodges and Dave Peacock (Chas and Dave) quoted with kind permission of Snout Music LTD.

I'll Never Walk Alone words and music by Richard Rodgers and Oscar Hammerstein © 1945, reproduced by permission of EMI Music Publishing Ltd, London W8.

Joanna Simmons and Jay Curtis have asserted their right under the Copyright, Designs and Patents Act 1988 to be identified as the authors of this work

First published in Great Britain in 2009 by
Square Peg
Random House, 20 Vauxhall Bridge Road,
London SW1V 2SA

www.rbooks.co.uk

Addresses for companies within The Random House Group Limited can be found at:
www.randomhouse.co.uk/offices.htm

The Random House Group Limited Reg. No. 954009

A CIP catalogue record for this book
is available from the British Library

ISBN 9780224086257

The Random House Group Limited supports The Forest Stewardship
Council (FSC), the leading international forest certification organisation.
All our titles that are printed on Greenpeace approved FSC certified paper carry the FSC
logo. Our paper procurement policy can be found at http://www.rbooks.co.uk/environment

Mixed Sources
Product group from well-managed
forests and other controlled sources
www.fsc.org Cert no. TT-COC-2139
© 1996 Forest Stewardship Council
FSC

Typeset in Trinité by Palimpsest Book Production Limited,
Grangemouth, Stirlingshire

Printed and bound in Great Britain by
Clays Ltd, St Ives plc

For George, Dylan and Joe. With much love.

A a

ABSOLUTE BEGINNERS

There's no training or trial period for being a parent, and you can't transfer to a more suitable position in Accounts. The only thing that qualifies you and your partner for the job is a womb and a willie and being able to point the latter at the former.

Most of us, when childless, have experienced that moment when a friend gives you their new baby to hold and you let its head loll dangerously. You console yourself with the thought that when you have your own child, this will not happen. You'll be a natural.

Then you have your own baby. And you let its head loll dangerously. Of course you do, you don't know what you are doing. Not the foggiest. This is the craziest thing about being a new parent. Looking after a baby is such an utterly all-consuming, serious, *epic* task – we are talking about another human life here – and yet you are allowed to do it having never done it before. If I were going to attempt Everest, I'd probably have a crack at Snowdon first. But what's the parental equivalent? Get a cat before you get pregnant? Doesn't even come close to the full baby experience. Witness: cats piss in plastic trays full of grit. Admittedly, a baby would, too, if you left it there long enough without a nappy, but that's not widely held up as 'best practice'.

So forget kitty – there is little you can do to prepare. Your inexperience will shine through like a beacon of blithering from day one. You must learn everything, from washing to winding to dressing and feeding, and all while sleep deprived (you, not the baby). You may have a grip on some basics, like babies need their nappies changed, but are sketchy on the detail like, er, how often. So on the hour you will whip off a dry one and replace it with another equally dry one, to a chorus of wails from your infant, because you thought that's what you did. Clean nappies – good!

You also have to relearn what you have spent the previous thirty odd years doing reasonably well. Crossing the road, for instance. How terrifying! If your partner is there, you will send him out on a reconnaissance mission first and, as you gingerly edge the buggy's front wheel off the pavement, he must remain in the middle of the road, arms outstretched, a human shield. Secretly, you would be more comfortable with a police escort. Do new parents qualify for one? Just a couple of outriders on motorbikes? No?

Your hands will shake and your heart pound as you offer

your virgin breast to your wobbly-headed baby. You'll fiddle with nipple shields and fanny with Infacol. You'll repop poppers skew-whiff and fumble with tiny socks. You'll dress him in absurd outfits aged two weeks (that mini denim jacket and tiny trainers combo) when a sleepsuit would do fine and you'll need help from three other adults to insert him in a Baby Bjorn. And how are you supposed to get meconium off? It's like tar mixed with Superglue. Phew! This is hard.

There's an old Spanish proverb that goes 'Experience is not always the kindest of teachers, but it is surely the best'. Hmmm, possibly. You might assume that the experience you gained from baby number one would stand you in good stead for baby number two. Except by then, a few years have elapsed and you find you have to learn it all again, then apply it to a baby who behaves differently from the last one, while juggling the needs of a two-year-old. That's a totally new experience. Back to school with you . . .

ACTIVITIES – EXTRACURRICULAR

Reasons why you might sign your kids up:

1. All the other kids are going to Mini Mandarin, Tiny Twinkletoes, Kiddie Kung Fu and Public Speaking for Pre-schoolers. Quick, you'd better send yours too. You don't want them to miss out. (On what, you're not really sure.)

2. Be honest, these activities are not for your kids, but for you, trying to shake off the spectre of your deprived seventies childhood. Yes, they will have the opportunities for personal fulfilment that you never had, and if that means presenting them with a veritable smorgasbord of cultural and sporting activities until they find one thing they can win a trophy at, then so be it.

3. Extracurricular activities are an ace way to avoid having to actually interact with your child. Once they're kicked out of Flamenco at 6.30 p.m., it's just fishfingers, bath, bed – job done.

Don't worry if you just can't be arsed, though. Mozart didn't go to Piano Club, and he did all right.

ADVERTISEMENTS

'It wasn't my fault. I sat on the remote. It shouldn't have been left there. All of a sudden we were on ITV. I was confused, disorientated . . . And then he saw them. One after another. They kept coming, ad after ad, toy after toy . . . so hideous, so pointless, so overpriced . . . I'd just wanted to protect him! If only we could turn the clock back to those innocent days of CBeebies. But it's too late now . . .'

ALCOHOL

You are now most probably, by force of circumstance, an infrequent visitor to pubs. So infrequent, in fact, that when you do go, you never fail to comment on the extortionate price of a pint these days and the fact that, since the smoking ban, they now all smell of men's bogs. Despite the lack of opportunities for social drinking, however, alcohol may well still play a fairly significant role in your life as a parent. Maybe it's the pent-up frustrations of modern-day positive parenting. The fact that instead of gobbing off like Ian Paisley and banging your fists on the table at dinner time, you have to ask your child very nicely if he would perhaps like to try another piece of broccoli in exchange for a Freddo Frog. Or maybe it's just the stultifying tedium of it all. Kids in bed, another groundhog night in front of the telly. Just you and your partner, valiantly outdoing each other with the sheer banality of your conversational gambits. 'I had a Pret sandwich for my lunch today.' 'Oh really, darling? I bought three pairs of pants and a portable potty in Mothercare.' It might even be a tiny act of rebellion. You're drinking for the sheer hell of it. Sticking a metaphorical two fingers up at the notion of responsible parenthood. You may be holed up in the kitchen, cooking pasta for five and unloading the washing machine, but hey! you think to yourself, I'm still a free spirit! Yeah! I can even drink half a glass of Pinot Grigio at 6 p.m.! Put that in your pipe and smoke it, conventional society . . .

Whatever your reasons, when it's the tense, nervous headache of parenting you're suffering, you conveniently forget about the restorative powers of two Anadin, a cup of camomile tea and an early night. Instead, you speed-read your way through *The Gruffalo* in order to get the Shiraz cracked open by 7.05. Of course, you're not drinking alone – that would be dangerous. You call your mum for a chat while you're doing it. If you're crying with boredom because you can't contemplate spending yet another evening in the front room of 101 Dullsville Street with only your partner and Sarah Beeny for company, a glass or two of Sauvignon Blanc will most definitely make him, you, or at least her, seem tolerably interesting.

You will always regret it, too. Oh, for the days when you could pander to a hangover at work, slumped behind your computer screen, scoffing bacon butties with your eyes half-open. Now it's up at six with a thick head, a two-year-old despot stamping on your shins and three different packed lunches to make. It's so not worth it. Just put the bottle down and the kettle on. You know it makes sense.

ALPHABETTI SPAGHETTI

Spells nothing but a crap dinner.

ANXIETY: ONSET OF GENERAL, NON SPECIFIC

From the moment that blue line appears, your new companion anxiety will squeeze you by the aorta as it hounds you through pregnancy and beyond. Before, in your hedonistic past, you were rightly proud of your inability to give a flying fandango about anything. Oh yes, you lapped up *Dead Poet's Society* in the Sixth Form and decided *carpe diem* was the way to go, having fun, abusing your internal organs and recklessly spurning your chance to take out a boring pension or buy cheap property in 1996. The future was intangible, unreal, unimportant even. Now, with a growing life inside you, the future rudely interrupts your carefree reverie. Everything from gorgonzola to global warming, to the extra-strong Americano you couldn't resist this morning (oh yes, shit, especially that), and the fact that you STILL have no flipping pension will have you wide-eyed and twitching at all hours of the day and night.

Take a chill pill – you'll need it. As long as it isn't contra-indicated, of course.

ART AND CRAFT

You always start off with great intentions. Yesterday's eight-hour Wii bender is all in the past. You put it behind you and move on. Each day brings renewed hope for your parenting potential and a fresh resolve to engage your child in meaningful creative activity. Yes, maybe today's the day he'll swap *Balamory* for a bit of light basket weaving if you ask him nicely. It'll be good for the both of you. Won't it?

Um, probably not. The problem with activities, particularly of the arty or crafty variety, is that they promise so much and deliver so little. It always sounds as though it should be a tremendous amount of wholesome fun. No brain-frazzling screens, no brightly coloured plastic, no globally syndicated cartoon characters, no shin pads. Just you, your child, the kitchen table and some bog rolls. It could be a mutually rewarding time of inspirational bonding as you banter and problem-solve co-operatively to create a magnificent pirate's telescope. Yes, of course it could. But it's much more likely to be a mutually lack-lustre few minutes of frustration and disappointment as you bodge together a soggy bit of cardboard hokum.

You blame it on out-of-control capitalism. (Well, it's easier than blaming yourself.) When you were young, if you wanted a death-trap tinsel advent candle, you bleeding well had to watch Blue Peter and make one. The fun potential in a sheet of sticky-backed plastic and some double-sided Sellotape used to genuinely excite you, but then, so did the crappy game of Guess Who? you had for your fourth birthday. But how is your twenty-first-century child meant to enter into the spirit of fashioning a cardboard light sabre when he's already got a plastic one with integral flashing lights and head-slicing sound effects languishing at the bottom of his over-stuffed toy chest? The children of today are worldly wise. If they can tire of a £25 all-singing all-dancing remote control Lightning McQueen within half an hour of its purchase, how can they be expected to spend the day playing with an egg-box beetle? However enthusiastic you pretened to be about making a Tardis out of a cereal box, he'll be less than convinced. Reclaimed bottle-tops and Copydex no longer cut it in the ruthless world of consumerist twenty-first-century crafts. If it doesn't move, buzz or flash, the kids just aren't interested.

But it's not only about the product, of course. The magic

should be in the creating itself. Who cares what you actually make, as long as you've both had fun? Fun? Uh oh. You haven't felt this up-tight since waiting for your A-level results. You like to think you're usually quite laid-back – you only change your bed sheets once a month, for crying out loud – but a bit of glitter, a few tubs of Play Doh and a three-year-old at large in your kitchen–diner will have you practically whimpering with nervous exhaustion. And actually, you fret to yourself, this calendar for Granny does need to be good. Because it's a flipping present! For scary Granny! You find yourself snatching the paintbrush from your child and turning his exuberant splodges into something more aesthetically pleasing. You hold his wrist a little too firmly as he attempts to pour some glitter. And as for cutting out those flower shapes, there is NO WAY on God's earth you're letting him loose in the house with a pair of scissors. So, *you* get increasingly tense and controlling. He gets increasingly bored and disinterested. And Granny gets a rubbish calendar made by her thirty-seven-year-old-daughter-in-law when she'd much rather have a box of Thorntons. No, it's simply not worth the pain of having to prise sticky sequins off your kitchen tiles for the next four weeks. Do you really want to know what you can make with a loo roll, a Pritt Stick and some poster paints? A sodding mess, and bugger all else, that's what.

ATTACHMENT PARENTING

It works in Outer Mongolia. FACT. It works for tribes in South America. FACT. The Inuit really rate it. FACT. So pick up your baby, lash him to your breast and keep him there until he's four, OK? This is attachment parenting, and it's coming to an NCT group near you.

It's cracking stuff, this. Baby will feel safe, secure – well, attached, basically. He won't cry. (How can he, his face is sandwiched between two breasts?) He'll grow up confident and calm. (How many Inuit do you know that have gone on shoot-'em-up rampages round a Sixth Form College, eh? Exactly.) And you'll enjoy it, too . . . for the first ten minutes, until you try to wipe your bum without dangling your child perilously over the toilet bowl. Or until baby weighs 12lbs-plus. Or until you want to baste the Sunday roast.

It's true, where to put your baby once he or she is no longer conveniently contained within your womb is a real issue. Hence the market for door rockers, baby seats, baskets, buggies and Bumbos. For some, the answer is you don't put your baby down at all, you hold it. Most parents who select this option have read the *Continuum Concept*, the Bible of attachment parenting. Published in 1975 by Jean Liedloff, it was based on her research into the lifestyles of the Yequana people of Venezuela. Oh look, she said, they hold their babies continually and it's really nice, and they all look quite relaxed. But that was a) in the seventies, and b) in the rain forest.

Of course, it would be lovely to be at leisure to cuddle your baby all day long, just like the Yequana people, but those women didn't have to walk to Homebase to pick up a can of pure brilliant white before popping into the Post Office to sort out the car tax, vacuuming the landing and putting a spag bol on.

Co-sleeping is central to the *Continuum Concept*, too. You don't spend all day with your infant bandaged to your back just to throw him into a cot come 7 p.m. Oh no. The child shares your bed 'until leaving of their own volition (often about two years)'. Yes, after an enjoyable second birthday they will wander off towards their own room come bedtime with a sleepy yawn and say, 'Thanks, Mum and Dad, the co-sleeping's been great, but now I think it's time I went it alone. See you in the morning – seven thirty OK?'

These days, co-sleeping is an emotive issue, and while it works for some, it's a terrifying nightmare for others. Squashing, overheating, snoring and dribbling on your baby are all real dangers. And unless you have a very big bed, Dad's basically on the sofa or in the spare room for the next few years. Government advice is against it, too, especially if you've been drinking or taking drugs. Especially then.

Sadly, we do not live in tribes any more (shame, as it would be far easier to get a babysitter). We are not surrounded by supportive friends and relatives, happy to attach themselves to our infant when we need a break. So if you go down the attachment route in twenty-first-century Britain, expect to be attached, be very attached. Which can go from feeling like the most natural thing in the world to feeling like the most un-natural thing. After all, if God had intended us to hold our babies 24/7, wouldn't he have given us pouches?

Oh, and here's a final interesting aside. Jean Leidloff, like some other high-profile baby gurus, has no children, but, on the *Continuum Concept* website, it says that 'Jean also enjoys painting'.

ATTRACTIONS

When we were kids, the equivalent of today's 'attractions' were: going for a walk, Swingball in the garden, the playground, a stately home. If you were incredibly lucky, you might get taken to Longleat Safari Park at some point between your birth and your eighteenth. Few were. There were no attractions to speak of. You were forced to be resourceful, or bored.

Now, though, there is Monkey World, Ostrich World, Kitten World, Marmoset World and Mini-Train Farm Park and Play Centre. Once, when on holiday in Dorset, ever on the alert for a child-friendly, wet-weather activity, I noticed a road sign for Monktown and thought, Wow, a town full of monks, maybe we should take the kids there, they could learn to make mead or something. But it was just a town. No monks. Not one. But the point is, *that's* how ubiquitous attractions are today.

They cost a packet to get into, that's my first beef. Even the titchy ones. A couple of chickens and a slide does not a farm park make, but that won't stop the owner charging £5 for over twos and £6 for adults. Each has a unique selling point, too, but that is generally lost on your child, who will hurtle round the genuinely engaging exhibits – 'Ooh, look, Billy, did you know that shire horses can pull up to five tonnes?' – in order to head for the play area. If this is inside it usually smells of pissy straw and goat turd because it's right next to the petting zoo and there's very little decent ventilation. If it's outside, it's probably on some wind-blasted corner of derelict farmland, with the odd chicken-wire pen alongside the swings containing a desultory guinea pig or two. Having pedalled mini Massey Ferguson tractors into bales of straw for two hours and wandered aimlessly about the maize maze, you are forced to exit via the gift shop. Of course, the gift shop. No visit to anything is complete without a gift. It's the attraction's way of thanking you for coming. Only it isn't a gift in the true sense of the word, as you must pay for that glow-in-the-dark caterpillar or pterodactyl mask, and you must do so simply to make it back to the car without violence erupting between you and your kids. Total cost of outing – ooh, loads probably.

B b

BABYSITTING

Not sitting on your baby, or your baby sitting, but having your baby sat. God, how we all yearn for those precious child-free evenings out. But if you can't get your mum to do the honours, is it *really* worth the hassle? Unless your babysitter is closely linked to your family by DNA or other unbreakable ties and doesn't mind being taken shameless advantage of, it is almost impossible to leave the house until your babies and toddlers are sound asleep. If you have the audacity to try, they will have prolonged and hysterical screaming fits, clawing at your freshly be-tighted legs whilst you try to explain that yes, you are in fact a separate entity who needs to go out some-times without them, yes, *without them*, but that you will *come back*. It would also be above and beyond the call of duty to expect your common-or-garden babysitter, who may be either a friend or a random fifteen-year-old, to have to calm and cajole your children into bed, when they would rather be watching *Masterchef* or flicking through *Heat* magazine. They are only there to 'sit' and dial 999 if fire breaks out, after all.

So, feeling guilty already for having even asked a non-relative to help you out (it's taken you a few months to build up the confidence) you have to carry out the usual testing dinner/bath/story/bed routine, but at high speed, whilst at the same time ironing your frock, rustily applying a bit of slap, attempting not to ladder a third pair of tights, assembling some refreshments on your kitchen counter, and making small talk with the sitter who has already arrived. Your partner might conveniently have made himself scarce during this process, having retreated to the bathroom at 6.30 only to emerge an hour and a half later looking pretty much the same.

You finally get to whisper the last lullaby and tiptoe out of the house at 8.41, arrive at the restaurant, and then bolt your dinner whilst frequently checking your mobile and watching what you drink. (You don't want to interrupt the babysitter's meditative *Newsnight*-watching trance with an Oliver Reed on *Wogan* style entrance into the living room, after all.) Come 10.30, you leg it home after a hurried mouthful of tiramisu and an agonising ten-minute wait for the bill.

The whole evening has been an exhausting blur and you don't really know whether you enjoyed it or not. What you do know is that it's cost you dear. £20 to the fifteen-year-old for enabling you to sit in your local crap Italian eating over-priced pasta for an hour and forty minutes. Or, worse, if it's your friend, no financial penalty, but the moral obligation to reciprocate the favour next week. Bugger it.

BAD BIRTH GUILT

You were going to breathe your baby out into loving arms, not send your lower half up to the moon on its own personal epidural rocket while a Ventouse hoovered your child from within you. Never mind, the baby has been born. OK, it didn't go quite as planned, but the baby is fine and you will be, too.

Sorry, what was that? Come again? You don't agree. You aren't just relieved it's all over. You're feeling – here it comes – the big fat G word: GUILTY! Before you've even left hospital you're carrying a burden of guilt and failure with you, which will hang over you for days, weeks, years. It might even put you off having more children because, uh oh, you idiot, you did it wrong! You didn't have a home birth/water birth/Laura Ashley birth/vegan humanist birth or whatever flavour birth you requested in your birth plan. There was no Groove Armada playing in the background. Candles were not lit. Favourite T-shirts were not worn. Massaging did not occur, for anyone. No. There was screaming and monitors and blood and endless pushing. Doh! Loser! That's what everyone is thinking. What. A. Complete. Loser. When it comes to giving birth, you are the Eddie the Eagle of labouring women. Other mothers are laughing behind their hands at you. And yes, you're right, your worst fears are confirmed, you are now officially a Bad Mother. And not in the funky sense.

It's a shame, really, when you consider that as recently as 1935 around 450 women died for every 100,000 births. Today, it is 14 per 100,000. But survival is not enough. No longer terrified that we might die of puerperal fever, we have become anxious about the style in which we give birth, rather than crapping it over the outcome, as every other woman pre World War II used to. It's no longer enough that a woman can give birth without, you know, expiring, she must now do it with scented candles burning and bestriding a gym ball.

We also assume that because we can make choices about almost every aspect of our lives, we can do the same with birth. We are then desperately disappointed when that doesn't quite pan out. Which it often doesn't, because when it comes to childbirth, you can have preferences, a few options, certainly a best-case scenario, but that's it. You can say 'I'm having a home birth' until you're blue in the face, but when it comes to it, what you may in fact be having is a high-speed drive into hospital followed by an emergency C-section.

Bad birth guilt also stems from a pressure of expectation that operates between the sisterhood. An invisible league table exists among new mums. Those who had a baby while crouching on the living-room floor with only some Rescue Remedy and Radio 4 to help, zoom in at number one, while those who had the full intervention bells and whistles in – the shame – a hospital, crash to the bottom.

Pressure, pressure, pressure. Our culture has it all wrong.

We should be celebrating new mothers, regardless of how or where they had their babies. Any woman who has just been through the ordeal of childbirth should have the Queen shower her in £50 notes newly minted in her honour while the Corgies walk about on their hind legs, juggling and wearing little clown outfits, then vestal virgins should bathe her in ass's milk while feeding her truffles. She should not, on the other hand, be feeling bloody sodding guilty. About anything.

BAKING

There is cooking, and then there is baking.

Children have very little interest in the former, but a great deal in the latter. They will never ask, 'Can we make some hummus, Mum? Or a carrot salad.' They want to bake.

There's the obvious appeal of licking the bowl, which you can't begrudge a child, but beyond that, children have some sort of Pavlovian response to baking. It equates with safety and comfort. My mother gave me Mr Kipling jam tarts when I got in from school, but how my little childish heart would have sung if there had been a plump Victoria sponge, fresh from the oven, awaiting me. To a child, baking, unfortunately, says love.

This is problematic if baking fills you with dread; if, as for many women, making a banana loaf seems akin to alchemy. This is also problematic if you simply loathe the process. All that billowing flour and tedious mixing. Children trying to crack eggs or sieve icing sugar or control a blender on the fast setting. God, just give it to me, will you?

Don't panic, though. There are plenty of Baking Made Easy books and posh role models, bestowing sex appeal upon all this cakery. Jane Asher has a crisp, upper-class approach to baking, like it's something you just get on with, without a fuss, and really, so much nicer than anything you can buy in the shops, don't you agree? Whereas for Nigella Lawson, baking raises us to the status of domestic goddess, 'trailing nutmeggy fumes of baking pie in our languorous wake'. Mmm, fumey! She adds, 'One of the reasons making cakes is satisfying is that the effort required is so much less than the gratitude conferred.' She's obviously never tried to whip up a lemon drizzle with my two, then.

It's all rather 1950s, how we pick up our pinnies and wooden spoons in an attempt at maternal perfection. What is implied is that you are a good mother when you bake. Contributing muffins to the school cake sale marks you out as morally sound. A homemade cake at a child's birthday party is universally admired. A sponge iced garishly by your child for Father's Day will bring a tear to Daddy's eye.

Ah, the rightness of it.

A big garlicky bowl of hummus, on the other hand, just won't cut it.

BARNEY

The theme tune was used to torture prisoners in Guantanamo Bay. Says it all really . . .

BATTERIES . . .

. . . are not included. Shame.

BEDTIME

OK, parents, quick straw poll. Hands up who enjoys bedtime? None of you. Of course.

It's pitched in the manuals as a quiet time of bonding and intimacy; freshly bathed children all pink and dopey, snuggling into you for a story. In reality, it's the excruciating last hurdle between you and a few longed-for hours of freedom. The inevitability of bedtime makes it thoroughly crushing. If it's six o'clock, it must be start-running-the-bath time. Not cocktail time. Not catch-an-early-film-then-go for-a-Thai time. Bath time. As Big Ben strikes, across the land, weary parents traipse upstairs to start the bedtime cogs a-turning. Shepherding reluctant children into the bathroom. Bong! Peeling off their grotty trousers and grubby socks. Bong! Persuading them into the bath. Bong! Creeping up behind them with a flannel to wash their faces. Bong! Prufrock measured out his life in coffee spoons: well, I'm measuring out mine in baths and teeth-brushing and tedious bedtime stories, night after night after night.

Children can show a staggering lack of focus when it comes to getting ready for bed. Come on, kids, it's the same every night. Bath, wee, teeth, pyjamas, bish, bash, bosh. Then they can show a staggering amount of focus in concocting last-minute delaying tactics. They need a poo, just as you are about to turn the light out, which is a risky one to argue with. Or your eldest suddenly takes an uncharacteristically focused interest in the alphabet, something he's happy to ignore for the rest of the day. Or he needs Big Ted, or Medium Ted, or Mini Ted, who is downstairs, or in the car, or at Granny's house. Noooooooo!

Households up and down the country all march to roughly the same bedtime tune, but with infinite variations, all uniquely torturous, all tolerated by us adults because somehow they make 'it' happen. One friend has to tell her girls the same made-up story each night about Phillips the farmer, in which Phillips's farm gets flooded and he goes to the Local Authority shelter where he is given hot soup and a blanket. ('We are public-sector workers, after all,' she points out.) We permit elaborate systems to be devised by the kids, too. The original drink/story/light-out routine blossoms into two stories together in the big bed, then a final wee, but he doesn't wash his hands again now, he does that in the morning, then a further story and one page of his Doctor Who magazine in his room. Then tucked in. Then a drink of water, but only if it's fresh, not yesterday's. Then find Foxy. Unless it's Tuesday, which is a Panda day. Then a kiss, then a cuddle, then a kiss – in that order. Then put the night light on, then turn the main light off, wait a minute, wait a minute, only – repeat – only if the landing light is already on. Back you go, get it right. That's better.

And all of this while you are desperately tired, having already clocked up twelve hours of childcare, and can smell freedom, moments away. The Pinot Grigio is chilling in the fridge, *Uni Challenge* is on in half an hour. Nearly there, nearly there, nearly there. But tread carefully. Lose it in these last vital moments, snap now, and the house of cards you have carefully constructed since you put the plug in at 6 p.m. will come crashing down. Bedtime is a test of nerves, agility and strength.

Sometimes, just to amuse myself vaguely, I tell my eldest son to put himself to bed, as I can't be bothered. He looks at me with complete incomprehension, as if brushing one's teeth and inserting oneself between a mattress and a duvet were rocket science. Yet I find it so very easy. In fact, for large parts of the day, it's absolutely all I want to do.

BIRTH PLANS

When you are pregnant for the first time, about the only thing you can know about childbirth is that it's coming. The style, duration and detail is a bit of a lottery. In fact, a textbook birth comes but half the time. According to NHS maternity statistics for 2005-6, just 47 per cent of expectant mothers have a regular, uncomplicated labour. That's not great news for the other 53 per cent.

But there's one thing you can do, faced with all this uncertainty. You can draw up a plan. A birth plan. It's more than just a good excuse to look out your fountain pen and buy some quality A4 from Paperchase, it is a chance to take control. If I write it down, it will happen . . .

The ingredients of your birth plan will be positive and uplifting. Unfortunately, the reality of birth might be quite different.

Birth Plan	Reality
Soft lighting	Fluorescent lighting
Soft music	Radio 2 on quite loud (because that's what the midwives are listening to)
Soft surfaces	Firm bed you cannot move from because you are being monitored
Soft faces	Stern faces as numerous midwives and consultants go on and off shift and wonder why it's taking you so long to get this baby out – are you pushing properly?
Softening cervix	A cervix that refuses to budge beyond 4 cm, even after twenty-four hours of labour
Soft drinks	Nothing to drink – you just puke it back up
Soft toys for the baby, once it arrives	Soft toy? What soft toy? Forgot all about it . . .

For pain relief, you are opting for holistic, non-clinical methods. Unfortunately . . . oh, you get the idea.

Birth Plan	Reality
Breathing	Paracetamol (they also offer this to people who have been in car crashes – no, they don't, but labouring women need to toughen up)
A TENS machine	Gas and air, which either does nothing for you or makes you sound like Deputy Dawg and imagine that the midwife is Hattie Jacques, and an epidural, which rather rules out the 'active' birth you were hoping for. Still, it was active for the anaesthetist
Hypno-birthing	No Paul McKenna, just your husband staring into your face, wide-eyed with anxiety
The birthing pool	Sadly, the birthing pool was busy

Amid all this, your birth plan may become lost. That oh-so-important document, pored over for weeks, copied out in best and urgently thrust into the midwife's hand as you arrive on the ward, has become trampled by a stampede of specialists all craning to squint at your cervix. The plan has become splattered with blood and barf, ripped and torn, then lost under a pile of sodden incontinence pads. Before the birth, you clung to it as an emblem of your right to speak out, to direct and control your labour, to be in charge, but in the 'excitement' of delivery, it was revealed for what it was – just so many optimistic words. That's why, despite asking for Merchant Ivory to direct your birth, you got David Lynch. On a bad day.

BOREDOM – THE NEW DEFINITION OF

Watching paint dry is the old definition of boredom. To a mother, that would now be calming and relaxing. The new boredom is far more active. It's having too much to do, but all of it requiring no more than 13 per cent of your mental capacity to do it. It is days that stretch into infinity, from being sledge-hammered awake at 6 a.m., to hour upon hour of outrageous demands and constant activity until the prize you have tortured yourself by dreaming about all day – their bedtime – comes around. By which point you are so exhausted, numbed and grumpy, you can barely find your own ankle, and your treasured few hours of liberty can only be spent slumped on the sofa, like a crudely automated corpse, anaesthetising yourself with Merlot while people have plastic surgery on telly in front of you. How did it come to this?

Here are some particularly boring things about having kids:

- children refusing to get in the bath
- children refusing to get out of the bath
- children being 'too tired' to walk when you are at least half a mile from home
- bedtime

- hearing yourself saying to other parents that he or she is 'not normally like this'
- hearing yourself saying to other parents that he or she is 'over-tired'
- children asking 'what can we do now?'
- children asking 'are we there yet?'
- children saying 'I'm bored'
- children saying 'no'
- children saying 'why?'
- walking slowly, everywhere
- any conversation that starts 'let's pretend . . .'
- other mothers talking about their kids' lavatorial habits
- kids' lavatorial habits
- bedtime
- waiting for it to 'get easier'
- talking about how it hasn't yet 'got easier'
- bedtime

BREAST OR BOTTLE?

The parenting issue guaranteed to get society at large collectively frothing at the mouth. The milk of human kindness smells distinctly whiffy when it comes to judging women on this one. Breast-feed your two-year-old in a Harvester in Lowestoft, and you might as well join up with the local naked transsexual unicyclist and mount a travelling freak show. At least then you could charge people for gawping at you with loathing and disgust. Bottle-feed your two-week-old in The Joy of Lentils in

North London, however, and you'd do as well to strap yourself into some stocks on Islington Green and invite women in floaty skirts to pelt you with organic vine-ripened tomatoes. It's a no-win situation.

Of course, human breast milk is best for human babies and there are numerous websites and organisations dedicated to promoting this fact. (Rightly so, as the Office of National Statistics 2005 survey reveals that only 21 per cent of babies in the UK are still being breast-fed at six weeks.) They cite various benefits for offering the boob from birth, ranging from enhanced bonding, to increased immunity and resistance to allergies, higher IQs, lower risk of diabetes, and, a strange one this: *portability*. (The fact that your breasts conveniently travel with you and don't need their own separate baggage handlers hardly needs pointing out, one would have thought.) Breast milk tastes great, too! Apparently. Though, frankly, I think that's a claim too far. They don't need to compete with Coca Cola. Not yet, anyway. So, of course, for the most part, these are great reasons to breast-feed. Scientifically proven and extremely valid. Add to that the fact that your previously unremarkable 34A breasts will look and feel like footballs for six months, and it's a no-brainer. Isn't it?

Well, perhaps not. Because it's sometimes not quite as earth-motheringly fluffy and straightforward as some might suggest. Breast-feeding can be eye-wateringly painful. You could have cracked and bleeding nipples, thrush, blocked ducts, un-comfortable engorgement, or delirium-inducing bouts of mastitis. You might have to spend several days with half a melting Savoy cabbage honking down your bra. In those first few weeks, it can seem that your baby is permanently clamped to your chest, day and night, sucking the very life force out of you. And let's be honest, society hasn't really put its heart into supporting you. It's all mouth and no trousers, yelling 'BREAST IS BEST', then letting an overworked midwife on your post-natal ward push an illicit bottle of Cow & Gate onto you in your weakened post-birth torpor. Like Mr Nick O'tine himself. 'Come on, love, just one. It won't matter. You know you want to.' Your GP may well advise 'topping up' with formula at the first hiccup in your baby's weight gain, and your local shopping centre will kindly suggest that if you really insist on breast-feeding, you'll have to do it on the bog.

So it's not that surprising that many women don't make it past that all-important six-week milestone, or don't even start at all. If only we did we'd know it gets much easier after those tricky early weeks. So much easier, in fact, that at four months you can feed your baby in the much admired one-armed rugby ball position, whilst running for the bus, eating an ice-cream. Until society gets its act together to educate its members and support new mothers with their feeding decisions, however, it almost seems that we're going to be damned if we do, and royally buggered if we don't. It's a choice of the Hobson's variety.

BRIBES

Frowned on in politics and the world of commerce, but with kids, the fastest way to get results. It's amazing what they'll do for a Chupa Chup. Call it a reward if it makes you feel better.

C c

CAPITALISM

During your angry youth, you may have flirted dangerously with extreme left-wing politics. Perhaps you blatantly sported an 'I heart Lenin' badge on your knee-length cardie, or joined a coach trip to London to swear under your breath at policemen from a safe distance in the 1990 poll tax riots. Once you have a child, however, unless you remove yourself immediately to a small croft in the Outer Hebrides, you will be making an irreversible pact with capitalism. Your consumption will rocket. You may have a slightly grubby feeling about it, deep down. A little moral discomfort in your bowels. You know that there are millions of people starving and children knitting trainers in sweat shops in the Third World, but you still feel compelled to buy twenty-four pairs of cute tiny animal-print socks and that remote-control cot mobile. You think your child might be disadvantaged if you don't get him a baby 'gym', even though putting him on a rug under the washing-line on a windy day would be just as effective. A tidal wave of useless crap will now torrent through your life, from Moses baskets to room-temperature alarms, bigger cars and bigger houses. You'll be bamboozled by a barrage of brand names. Yes, it turns out your suspicions were correct. A Bugaboo™ is just a £700 garish fashion accessory on wheels. A Likeabike™ is indeed, like a bike, but twice the price for two fewer pedals. Kandoo™ wipes are the same as wet bog roll, and a Sangenic™ Nappy bin, is, well, a bin. Enough said. As your children grow, you'll get through so many brightly coloured by-products of the Chinese petro-chemical industry that you'll feel person-ally responsible for global warming. And it's not just *your* capitalist tendencies. Raised in a rampantly consumerist society, your children exhibit the ruthless materialism of Gordon Gecko, but with slightly less compassion. 'Greed is good, isn't it, Mummy?'

So what can you do? You can make your child look like a hippy throw-back freakazoid by refusing to let him watch adverts and swapping some courgettes from your allotment for some artisan-carved wooden toys. My, he'll be popular for playdates! Or you can jump onto the conveyor belt of consumerism, hand over a blank cheque to Toys R Us and buy an obscene amount of stuff over the next ten years (together with a big new house to fit it all in).

But don't despair just yet. It's OK. You can assuage your capitalist guilt whilst still spend, spend, spending. Phew! Just consume and campaign at the same time. Take a leaf out of Bono's book. It's fine to have a personal wealth greater than the GDP of the Gambia, as long as you repeatedly tell everyone else to get off their arses to END WORLD POVERTY. Shout FEED THE WORLD, and go and buy that four-wheel drive. Maybe you can have it all.

CAREFUL

How many times a day do you say it? And how many times do they listen? It's like traffic noise to children – they just zone it out. Careful, careful, careful, broom, broom, broom . . .

You could also try 'mind!'.

CAR JOURNEYS

The only good thing about a car journey is that your children are physically, but legally, restrained and, unless you have been particularly careless, are safe from paedophiles/ nettles/wasps/big boys who won't share, once inside the car. So in some ways you can relax.

In all other ways you cannot. Car journeys with kids are rich with uncertainty. Will they sleep, not sleep, puke, mutiny on the M5? Will you toss all sensible driving theory out of the window and find yourself taking spectacular risks, deciding that it's much better to swerve dangerously as you grope behind your seat for the dropped Buzz Lightyear than to listen to a kiddie chorus of car-based cakka for the next twenty-seven miles? Will you also deem it better, despite the negative effect on your concentration, to paw for that multi-bag of Quavers on the seat beside you, carefully undo a packet at the wheel then pass it back to your child, all the while staring madly ahead of you at the road, wide-eyed, trying to concentrate on the caravan in front, which is weaving a bit, when really you're just visualising your hand, the Quaver packet, where their hand is, have they got it, will they spill them? Yes? No?

Of course, the Highway Code does not prepare you for car journeys with kids. What to do when you approach a box junction – yes. What to do when your child has wriggled out from his seat straps and keeps opening his window, so it sounds as though a chopper is landing on the car roof – no.

To add to your woes, with tedious predictability, someone will need a wee and there is no service station for thirty-two miles. Hard shoulder it is. Sadly, in pulling onto the hard shoulder you have pulled onto the *shoulder of death*, because these are notoriously treacherous bits of road on which to park – around 250 people are killed or injured on them every year. If you do stop on one, you're all meant to immediately get out of the car and clamber as far away from the road as possible *even*, yes, *even* if it's raining. Not leave the rest of the family in the Focus as you dangle your two-year-old over the Tarmac while Polish lorries thunder past at seventy miles per hour.

Mind you, car journeys have come a long way, as it were. Back in the good old days, when we'd take the Cortina down to Devon for a week, Father would smoke the entire way, filling the car with unfiltered Dunhill fumes while I vomited regularly onto my teddy. It would take my mother so long to pack the car (no help from Dad who was reading the paper – well, it was the seventies) that we would leave four hours late and have to stop for our crab paste sandwiches in a lay-by approximately seven miles from home. There was no in-car entertainment either. No mini versions of favourite games or nursery rhyme CDs. It was I Spy or nowt. One thing has remained constant, though, when it comes to car journeys: children still ask, 'Are we there yet?'

No, children, we are not.

CHANGING BAG

Otherwise known as an Abnormally Expensive Bag, the specialist Changing Bag is one of those things you never knew you needed. Then you buy it and find out you don't. You persevere for the first nine months of your baby's life, filling the multifarious pockets with all manner of ephemera; seven nappies, two packs of wipes, two changes of clothes, three muslins, three dummies, rice cakes, Tupperware pots of fruit, first-aid kit, anti-depressants, cuddly toys. Oh yes, you're certainly prepared for any eventuality on your daily struggle out of the house with what appears to be a para-chute pack straining on the handles of your buggy. Trouble is, in your newly insular environment, your daily routine of an hour in the park, followed by coffee and cake and a whistle-stop tour round the Co-op doesn't really necessitate emergency precautions. You're lucky if you get through a couple of rice cakes and a wipe. And that's only to keep the baby quiet while you eat your chocolate muffin in the café and to clean the crumbs off your hands afterwards.

You gradually realise that you are carting the same crap around with you day after day in a completely futile attempt at efficient mothering. The individual pouches of the bag are no good to you because you can't remember what's in them. You rarely open them and when you do it's like scraping the bottom of a festering mini-bin, full of soggy biscuit crumbs, fluffy raisins, broken crayons and 13p in coppers. The bottle holder looks like a bottle holder it's true, but if you're breast-feeding it's just a ridiculously oversized breadstick container and makes you look like a twat. You've rejected the integral vacuum-packed changing mat because you can't be arsed to unravel it, or even to change the nappy until you get home. You're only ten minutes away, after all! No – enough is enough. You decide to chuck out the changing bag. What you need is a *normal bag*. A little bag. A cheap bag, or maybe an old bag. Some wipes, some rice cakes, your keys and a tenner. There now. You're prepared for whatever motherhood may throw at you.

CHEESE STRINGS

On the packet it says they are 100 per cent natural. But what other cheese do you know that can be fashioned into a palm tree?

CHILDCARE

Let's break down your choices, so you can make an informed and confident decision.

Nanny. The SAS of the childcare world – highly trained, super fit. Only for big girls who do proper jobs, five days a week (or the moneyed elite, who need time off to get their nails done). Cheaper if they live in, pricier if they live out, really expensive whichever way you slice it. They will not hang up your washing or do the ironing. Your child may call them Mummy.

Au pair. The knock-off version of a nanny, at a fraction of the price. Usually barely out of nappies themselves. Obliged to do some 'light' housework, but may not know how to unload a dishwasher. They will only work a handful of hours each week and must live in, therefore there is some risk they will have an affair with your husband.

Childminders. Women who need to make staying at home with their own kids more lucrative. May offer your child vital one-to-one attention, but may also take him/her to Sainsbury's and on the school run. Home from home for junior? Or a piss-take at £5 per hour?

Nurseries. Currently the most popular form of non-parental care in this country, but the whipping boy of the childcare world. You can read a scare story a week about how nurseries will screw your child over. Research carried out in the US found that children who go to nursery are more likely to be aggressive and disruptive once they reach school. This persists until the age of twelve. And it doesn't matter how good the nursery is, either. Still, the study also found that nursery attendees were more articulate at the age of ten. So they may commit acts of aggression willy-nilly across the playground, like Genghis Khan in grey shorts and an Aertex shirt, but they'll be able to tell you all about it later.

You need to think about cost, of course. They are all expensive. If you're lucky, you will get to keep a quarter of your net income. Some women even lose money each month after paying childcare, but do it to keep their place at work. What a great reason to get out of bed each morning . . .

So there are your choices. Perhaps choices is too strong a word. A set of compromised options which involve you handing over 80 per cent of your earnings for the chance to feel vaguely uneasy three days a week. Yes, that's more like it.

CHOKING

The heightened fight-or-flight response mode of parenthood has, of course, evolved for good reason. For all our somewhat overplayed fears of catastrophic see-saw accidents and abduction by celebrity paedophiles, a constant state of parental orange alert is actually required because of what Freud described as the child's *oral fixation*. Or, in other words, its Darwinian compulsion to remove itself from the gene pool by shoving all objects with which it comes into contact into its mouth. And, sometimes, down its windpipe. Given the chance, a small child will gleefully imbibe and inhale gravel, cat biscuits, golf balls, dog poo and bleach. My interest on this topic stems from 1975 when I decided to block my trachea with a miniature Playmobil plastic basket. My trachea (fortunately) recovered, but my nerves, alas, did not.

Take my advice. If you're of a nervous disposition, purée everything your child eats until it is five.

And when it comes to whole grapes, be afraid, be very afraid.

COMPETITIVE PARENTING

We're not talking about parents trying to outsmart and outdo other parents by giving their kids Latin lessons aged one or by going on posher holidays or to wankier hotels than their posh wanky neighbours, although that does go on, but mainly in North London so, you know, whatever. We're talking about the mum and dad within the same parental unit competing with each other.

It happens most in the first year of your child's life. It's because with a new role in the household – that of primary carer – comes the need to define that role and explain it, otherwise the non primary carer might just assume that it's a piece of cake. So, if you are the primary carer you become obsessed with making sure your partner knows, *really* knows and understands, what you are going through. The non primary carer in return must state his case and defend his right to be just as tired or anxious or bored as you are. He can't be outdone by his partner just because she happens to find herself in an absurdly testing new role. Ding ding, round one – you're off!

Popular competitions between new parents are: who is most tired, who has the harder job, who needs time out more and who is most stressed.

They go something like this . . .

Mum: I'm really tired today.
Dad: I've been really tired all week.
Mum: Actually, I'm not tired, I'm exhausted.
Dad: I'm profoundly weary.
Mum: I'm chronically sleep deprived. I'd like to be just weary, but I'm way beyond that. Being weary is like a fond, distant memory to me.
Dad: Yeah, well, I'm so weary, I make Leonard Cohen look like The Cheeky Girls.

And so on and so forth.

These are competitions that no one can win. Having a young child is hard on everyone. So, parents, pull together, not apart. Make love, not war, or at the very least just, um, be nice to each other. And if you can't be nice, do what they did in the war: Keep Calm and Carry On.

CONTROL

Call me a loony paranoid conspiracy theorist if you will, but it seems to me that from the moment that positive pregnancy test result appears, women may begin to experience a peculiar sensation akin to that felt by democracy-loving avant-garde poets in Cold-war East Germany. That is, the slightly disturbing feeling of being WATCHED. Of being JUDGED. And of being CONTROLLED. OK, so maybe consuming half a glass of Champagne and a reheated prawn wonton whilst pregnant at the office Christmas party won't get you mind-fucked by the Stasi, but it certainly will give sticky-beak Sue in Human Resources a valid reason to gossip about you malevolently to all and sundry. She has every right to do so, of course, because your body is no longer your own. It belongs to Society at Large now. You are merely hand-maid to The Man. Pregnancy and motherhood seemingly give Government and Society a handy opportunity to pull an increasingly wayward section of the population (that's you and me, sister) back into line.

But can you blame them? Bloody upstart women. Taking jobs in middle management! Politely requesting equal pay! Brazenly drinking lager and laughing amongst themselves in pubs! Occasionally asking for help with unloading the dishwasher! No wonder The Man was getting concerned. His solution was to Confuse and Conquer. To re-load society's ammunition for judging women and putting pressure on them to conform by bombarding them with endless (and often inconsistent and conflicting) rounds of information and 'advice' during pregnancy and beyond into motherhood. Information should, of course, give women the freedom to make educated choices, but making that information so complex just seems to make them come over all unnecessary. How convenient.

So, as it goes, once pregnant, you apparently relinquish your right as a human being to run for the bus, clutching (with intent) a double-espresso and a tuna-mayo sandwich. You can now forget about that only glimmer of fun on the horizon of pregnancy tedium because The Man has metaphorically whipped your Friday glass of wine away from your expectantly puckered lips and chucked it down the sink, tutting disapprovingly. No matter that there is no statistical evidence to suggest that a couple of units of alcohol a week would harm your foetus. Apparently, women are too dim to understand that two units doesn't, in fact, mean two bottles of Thunderbird, and so must be told not to touch the stuff at all in case of 'confusion'. Doh.

OK, so obviously excessive alcohol, drug and cigarette intake is BAD. Even my cat knows that. And he's pretty stupid. But you must now also view a multitude of seemingly innocuous substances and activities with dark suspicion. Don't forget, behind every slightly oozing Camembert and session of light weeding lurks a sinister menace. It doesn't matter that you are four times as likely to give birth to triplets as you are to get Listeriosis whilst pregnant. Just step away from the Stilton (and buy three cots). The Man is undermining your ability to evaluate risk effectively and make sensible decisions. You're caught like a rabbit in the headlights. Should you cross that really busy road to get your organic hummus sandwich, or should you stay safely on this side and chance the Brie baguette?

Maybe you'd be better off staying at home.

Then there's the birth itself. You may imagine yourself bellowing like a serene bovine goddess as you wallow on all fours in a pool listening to plinky-plonky music, but The Man would much prefer to have a hand in it, if not a large pair of forceps and a sharp pair of scissors. And once your baby is born he will tell you to co-sleep, then not to co-sleep, you thrill-seeking danger monkey. He will encourage you to go back to work, but will then tell you that nursery is turning your little angel into a little Hitler. And an obese one to boot.

Oh, I don't know, maybe The Man is really just concerned for our welfare, for our babies and our children. Maybe he cares.

Or maybe he's a giant lizard who is MESSING WITH OUR HEADS.

At least, that's what David Icke told me.

COOKING WITH YOUR COAT ON

You come in and there's just no time to take it off. There's no let-up. One activity plunges at high speed into the next, like a sadistic Newton's Cradle. So before you can say 'I'll just take my coat off' you've got a boiling pot on the stove, an onion chopped, cans opened and grillable food grilling, you've given them both a drink and turned Cartoon Network on to buy you extra seconds and you're listening to your voicemail messages while opening the post. Spectacular! If a bit warm. Because you're still wearing your coat.

CRANIAL OSTEOPATHY

You may not have been a consumer of alternative therapies before the arrival of your child. Perhaps you were even actively cynical about them, confident in your opinion that the petals of the winter-blossoming Chinese mallow spunkflower cannot, in fact, cure cancer. But once your baby is born and once it cries for more than ten minutes, you start to cast about for help. This crying cannot go on. Something must be done. Something *alternative*.

Mention it to even the sanest of sane people and they'll immediately whip out a card for Dr M. T. Bank, Cranial Osteopath, and urge you to make an appointment. You decide to give it a shot, even though they might just as well recommend you visit a baby levitation technician or expert in infant chakra realignment. It doesn't matter. The randomness of placing all your hope in somebody manipulating your tiny baby's head in a series of so-small-as-to-be-invisible fingertip moves is lost on you, morphed as you have from rational adult into panicky, try-anything parent.

After a course of six sessions at £35 a time, your baby does seem a bit more settled. Maybe cranial osteopathy really is the key to calmer babies. Or was he due to get over his colic around now anyway? We'll simply never know . . .

CRUELTY . . .

. . . in kids. 'Eve is much prettier than you, Mum.' Oh, thanks very bloody much. She's also four, you know, so give me a break.

. . . in parents. Withholding biscuits. Because you can.

CRYING

Apparently, a mother can subtly distinguish between her child's cries to help her correctly respond to his needs. Here's how:

Type of cry	Interpretation
Alarming high-pitched sob first thing in the morning	Mum, I'm really hungry
Alarming high-pitched sob maybe at lunch time	Mum, I'm really hungry
Alarming high-pitched sob whilst a smell of the farmyard pervades the atmosphere	Mum, I've pooed my pants
Alarming high-pitched sob in park	Mum, I've just dropped my ice-cream
Alarming high-pitched sob at 6 p.m. whilst rubbing eyes	Mum, I'm over-tired
Alarming high-pitched sob not identified as one of the above	Mum, you think I'm teething but I'm actually just really upset that I can't get my foot in my mouth

Similarly, an advanced partner might be able to distinguish between the cries of his child's mother:

Type of cry	Interpretation
Desperate gulping sob	I don't know why the baby's crying
Desperate gulping sob	I can't bear the baby crying any more
Desperate silent sob	I'm really quite tired
Desperate silent sob with no tears	I'm too tired to cry
Desperate hysterical sob	I'm over-tired
Desperate yelping sob	My nipples feel like Satan's marshmallows

D d

DAD COMPARISONS

There's always a dad out there who's more slack, more hope-less, more late in more often than the one who fathered your kids, which somehow means you're not supposed to complain.

DADS COMPLAINING ABOUT BEING THE BREADWINNER

What? Shut up! You love going out to work. All of you do. It's the great unsaid. You love being able to walk away. No? Well, you look after them, then, if it's so jolly tempting.

DAD EXCUSES

'I didn't get the kids up because I didn't hear them. I was asleep, so it's not my fault.' No, and it's not my fault that I'm programmed to hear them and unable to lie there while they yell. Not my fault, but grinding me down all the same. Is your not-your-fault grinding you down as much as my not-my-fault? Only it looks like yours helps you get more rest than mine does.

DAD GLAMOUR

You're the primary carer, but as soon as Dad walks in, wow, they're cheering like it's snowing giant party bags stuffed with Gogos and fluffy kittens. Now, to quote my four-year-old, that's not fair.

DADS NEEDING TO LET THEIR HAIR DOWN

It's not his fault that a quiet drink turned into a bender and he didn't bother to ring you. It's also not his fault that he was so appallingly hungover the next day he was unable to participate in family life, transforming your weekend into a busman's holiday of epic proportions. Guys need to get away from it all sometimes, you know? Forget all about kids and responsibilities and shit. The fact that he is an immature eejit? Now that *is* his fault.

DAD OUTFITS

Men can dress themselves, but not their children. A T-shirt in winter, last year's tiny socks, they look *fine*. Yes, that vest is a touch tight now, making your three-year-old son look like he's about to jump up and sing 'YMCA', but not to worry. And he wants to wear his sandals, even though it's February, and Dad gives a thumbs-up to that. Wearing the appropriate shoes for the season is just so last season. Dads understand these things.

DEPRESSION – POST-NATAL AND OTHER ASSORTED MISERIES

Just like the yin and the yang, the joyous highs of parenting co-exist in a complex symbiotic relationship with some staggeringly crushing lows. Even if you're an annoying glass-half-full sort of person and spend a lot of time living it large with your yang, when it comes to embarking on the life journey of having kids, your previously unassuming yin might just turn around and rob your handbag whilst pushing you into the nearby Pit of Despair.

About one in ten mothers will suffer from post-natal depression at some point and the same number will experience the less widely recognised ante-natal variety. About one in five hundred develop the far more serious post puerperal psychosis. Man, that's a lot of miserable mothers. So what's going on? Why are so many of us psychologically devastated by what should be the most amazing event of our lives?

In the past, our very *femaleness* has been blamed for our maternal melancholia. Probably by twatty misogynist toffs in white coats. Oh yes, don't worry your little head, dear, it's just your hormones making you want to hurl your baby out of the window. That sort of thing. But current research demonstrates that hormone levels in depressed mothers are often the same as those in content mothers. Experts now point the finger of blame for triggering maternal depressive episodes squarely at major *life changes*. And indeed, child-rearing experiences tally up pretty convincingly on that front:

1. Undergoing a complete transformation of your body and lifestyle. TICK.
2. Having a violent and bloody experience of childbirth, akin to that of being involved in a serious road traffic accident. TICK.
3. Having to assume full responsibility for a tiny helpless being where before you've only looked after a goldfish. TICK.
4. Losing sleep. TICK.
5. Losing your freedom. TICK.
6. Losing your sex-drive. TICK.
7. Losing your social life. TICK.
8. Losing your identity, LOSING YOUR KEYS, **LOSING YOUR MIND!!! TICK. TICK. TICKETY BLOODY TICK.**

Frankly, it's astonishing that we're not *all* sitting on the stairs in our pyjamas, glassy-eyed and rocking, chewing on a muslin.

But there is some good news about being depressed in 2009. (That's as opposed to being depressed in 1959, of course, not

as opposed to not being depressed at all. That would be silly!)
In the old days depression was quite the taboo. Women suffered
in silence all day then got shouted at by their husbands when
they arrived home to find no dinner on the table. If your doctor
ever did take you seriously instead of just patting you on the
hand and recommending you cheer yourself up with a new
hairdo, he would send you off for a bit of Electroconvulsive
Therapy. After a few hefty shocks to the brain, you may still
have been depressed, but at least you would have forgotten
why. And your own name, probably.

These days, thank goodness, depression is really out and
proud. At least, you're not alone. You can't pick up a Sunday
supplement without reading an account of someone's PND. It's
comforting to know that even Fern Britton and Angelina Jolie
have been there, too. Isn't it? And although there's a lot of help
and treatment available to the twenty-first-century depressed
mother – talking therapies, support groups, help-lines – it's the
wide range of anti-depressant medication available that is
the biggest difference. Now, unencumbered by the burden of
embarrassing taboo, women are bonding over their SSRIs of
choice. Will it be the Seroxat, the Prozac or the Citalopram? The
weight gain, the restless legs or the furry mouth?

God, it's enough to make you depressed . . .

DINNER

Not theirs silly, yours!

Once a pleasant but innocuous daily pastime for you and

your partner, having dinner together used to be a fairly straightforward matter of having nice food out, having nice food in, grabbing a takeaway, or tucking into yesterday's leftovers on your lap in front of *The Bill*. A bit of sustenance and a bit of a chin-wag. Normal, healthy human behaviour.

Once you become a parent, however, all this changes. Having dinner à deux assumes the significance of a mysterious ritual in a religious sex cult; something strangely exciting in which you rarely participate, but which is worthy of an entry with two exclamation marks on your calendar. Followed by a crap shag.

Maybe you don't actually eat together much these days. Perhaps one of you gets to luck out on the burnt fishfinger and unsalted broccoli duty with the kids, whilst the other has an appointment with the microwave every evening at 8 p.m. Maybe you all dine together in a family tableau that nods more towards the Adams than the Waltons. Whatever your usual scramming arrangements now, though, they seem to foster the feeling that, as a parent, dinner alone with your partner is no longer just dinner. Dinner is now Sacred. Dinner is Freedom and Independence. It is Fun and Intimacy. It is a Right Royal Rogering on a very full stomach. Forget the youthful fripperies of drink'n'drugs'n'rock'n'roll. Dinner is how you get your parental rocks off. Yeah, that's 8.30, Thursday, window seat, Donatello's. BRING IT ON!!!!

Conferring such elevated meaning and status onto the act of scoffing down a bit of grub without your children at 8.30 p.m. on a week night can cause a few problems, of course.

First there is the tedious strategic planning of it all. Never forget, this is a SPECIAL OCCASION! Dinner for two may now be many things to you, but spontaneous it is not. Get yourself a BlackBerry. There are babysitters to court, tables to be booked, taxis to be ordered and fancy pants to be purchased. Then there's the crushing weight of expectation. It's your first time out together for six months, it's your fortieth, his forty-first, you've got a new kitten, William and Kate have just tied the knot and you've managed at last to book a table in that restaurant that appeared on *Ramsey's Kitchen Nightmares*. Oh yes, this is special. As special as it gets.

But with all that pressure to have fun, intimacy and romance, a £120 bill, and a 10.30 curfew to boot, the odds of you having a memorably great evening are well and truly stacked against you. You'd have been better off going to the pub and getting some chips on the way home. No more pan-frizzled halloumi gribbles and tense conversation. Just a bit of sustenance and a bit of a chin-wag. And a bit of a shag. If you're lucky.

DIRTY SECRETS

In the safe, neutral territory of the playground, at the school gates or picking them up from nursery, we can all do a convincing job of looking like normal, capable, on-it parents. But behind closed doors, in almost every household, lurk dirty secrets. We never meant them to happen. We should have tackled it sooner . . . He has chocolate milk from a bottle.

She's started school, but still has a dummy at night. I let them watch three hours of TV a day because I don't want to play with them. I still spoon-feed him his dinner, and he's five, just because . . . For *shame!*

DISAPPOINTMENT

Your kids will disappoint you. They respond inappropriately and behave inappropriately at inappropriate times. They're never quite grateful enough. And they like rubbish food.

DOING TOO MUCH FOR THEM

We tailor our lives to our children. At weekends, we do what they want. We are terrified of their dissent, so instead of taking them to the supermarket we shop online or exhaust ourselves by going at 11 p.m. at night, rather than risk their disapproval in the cereal aisle of Sainsbury's. And so we shelve the mundane tasks of daily life or hurriedly complete them while the kids are at school or nursery, to do what? To free up time so we can take them to soft-play places or 'attractions'.

When I was a kid, my parents would go to the pub on Saturday lunch time. My brother and I were left in the car with a bottle of shandy each and a packet of cheese and onion crisps, while they disappeared into the warm, smoky comfort of a child-free boozer. Occasionally, my mum would weave across the gravel car park, tap on the window, and mouth 'You all right?', before gliding back to her sherry. And we didn't mind. We just accepted it. One pub we went to even had a swing.

These days, you wouldn't leave your kids in the car in case somebody reports you to Social Services. Instead, you choose only to visit pubs with theme parks built in their gardens, so that you can enjoy a hurried pint while standing in the cold, overseeing your kids on the slides and breaking up fights. You do it to make yourself feel like you're still having a life. Look, you're saying, I'm at the pub, it's cool, everyone's happy. But in fact, it would be easier and less frustrating to go to the park with a four-pack.

And don't get me started on holidays. Some adults I know – and these are educated, sentient, interesting people – actually take their kids to Disneyland Paris for their annual holiday. I mean, for fuck's sake. In what possible way is this a holiday – for anyone. Of course you'll loathe it, but you might just extract some small soupçon of pleasure from the whole commercialised tack-fest if you feel your kids are loving every minute. But they won't. They'll get over-tired and pissed off when they can't buy yet more Coke and/or gift-shop hokum, and you will all return home somewhat confused, exhausted and perhaps ever so slightly ashamed. As if you'd taken a tab of acid and shown your tits to a pensioner. What was that all about? you'll think later. Why did I do that? And how demeaning.

We certainly do too much for our kids. It's because we care. But it's also because we're soft and a bit scared of them. And as we don't expect them to come to the supermarket and the

DIY shop and the tip at the weekend, we have to do *something* with them. It's questionable how much they benefit from our generosity, too – surely the final irony? So bring back the system of benign neglect that our parents championed. Put parents' needs back on the family agenda, and tell Monkey World where to shove its bananas.

DRESSING

Many women who have yet to make the quantum leap into motherhood have a morning routine that involves a certain amount of gazing into their wardrobe pondering what to wear, a leisurely application of make-up while the *Today* programme hums in the background, perhaps even a once-over with the hair straighteners. But once children have arrived on the scene, with all their many and fascinating requirements ready to kick in from the moment their eyelids pop open, dressing is not something to spend time over. It is something to be achieved.

This can lead to rush jobs. Yesterday's top is still out so pop it on then realise once you're out of the house that it has a snail trail of snot, left by your youngest, streaked across its shoulder. There's probably some encrusted yogurt on the crotch of your jeans, too, but do your coat up and no one will guess. You're not quite going out with your pants on your head – things haven't got that bad yet – but grooming this ain't.

To help, many women simplify their dressing by creating a capsule wardrobe, which is another way of saying a uniform.

That's jeans and boots if it's raining; jeans and sandals if it's fine. Simple. Add coat in winter, leave off in summer. If you find yourself with a bonus ten seconds to spare before you hurtle into the day, you can apply a wisp of mascara, which may fox the untutored eye into thinking you're slightly more awake than you feel. Et voilà. Away you go.

DRUDGERY

Washing up, tidying, laundry, tidying, cooking, wiping bums, tidying, tidying, tidying.

E e

EARLY

Your definition of early will change and become fluid once children are part of your life. Before you have them, 7 a.m. is early. Wow! 7 a.m.! That's practically a lie-in now. As for proper weekend lie-ins, these days, 8.30 is the new 11 a.m. You can feel positively bionic on an 8.30.

Adjusting your concept of early is critical to surviving life with children. You have to start seeing your child staying in bed until 6.45 as an achievement, not a gross infringement of your right to sleep. You must tell yourself a 6 a.m. start is OK from your eight-month-old because, hallelujah, she slept through. Then, as she gets older, this 6 a.m. may become a wholly civilised 6.35 a.m. and you will feel like you've won the lottery. You are institutionalised now, so have forgotten that pre kids you never got up at 6.35, not even to go on holiday. Don't feel too smug, though, because here comes the curve ball – the EARLY, early start. A sudden 5.15 a.m. kick-off – where the *hell* did that come from?

The problem with waking really early is that you are tired all day, in that itchy-eyed, tense-brained way. It shows in your face. It doesn't matter what time you went to bed, you will feel like a husk. Worse still, waking early can actually send you mad. It's not just the tiredness, it's the fundamental wrongness of being up when most of the population is still asleep. It's lonely. There are weird people on the radio. You don't know when to eat breakfast. You have no idea how you are going to get through the day.

What you do is pull the normal timetable of life forward by a few hours. Breakfast is over by 6.45. You're showered by 7.10 and everyone's dressed and ready to hit the park by 8. It does mean you'll have to eat lunch at 10.45 and everybody will be exhausted and testy by 12.15, but think of all the fresh air you'll have had.

EDUCATION

Not theirs, silly, ours! We all know how brilliant girls are at school. From their very first days, while the boys spend their time talking about farts and playing wildly complicated wrestling games, the girls are studiously practising their joined-up writing, effortlessly learning to read and saying good morning to you in French. And it just gets better. Girls are out-performing boys at GCSE level, they get more A grades at A level, and more of them make it to university. In 2002–2003,

58 per cent of first-year undergraduates were women. Wow! It's almost as if they were being educated to do the important jobs, like men!

But don't get too excited. The clock chimes midnight at this point and we all turn into pumpkins. The 2008 Equality & Human Rights Commission report *Sex and Power* reveals that our fabulously intelligent and educated sisters are missing out on all the top jobs. Women hold just 11 per cent of FTSE 100 directorships, only 19.3 per cent of the positions in Parliament, make up just 14 per cent of university vice chancellors, 13.6 per cent of editors of national newspapers and 25 per cent of heads of professional bodies. In fact, there has even been a drop in the number of women attaining key posts in Britain, with fewer female MPs, cabinet members, health service and local authority chief execs, senior police officers, judges and heads of professional bodies in 2007 than the year before.

It's no mystery. We all know why. We're clever, you see. We've had good educations and we didn't waste time in Reception having flobbing competitions when we should have been practising our Jolly Phonics. The small matter of us having ovaries and a womb – and wantonly using them – can instantly shave 50k and several management points off our job prospects. Team that with a long-hours, inflexible work culture designed for men, rubbish paternity leave and a distinct lack of good quality, affordable childcare and it's no wonder so few women make it to the top.

All that time and money spent on our educations, what was it for? Perhaps it was all part of society's plan to provide a

cultured and intelligent 'motherforce' to turn the next generation of wayward boy-children into high-achieving men. And if
we don't like it, there's only one thing to do. Keep schtum about
everything we have ever learnt and raise a generation of male
thickies. That way, our high-achieving sisters have a chance.
Mothers of the world unite! Forget everything you learnt about
Palladian architecture at university, deny all knowledge of the
past-historic tense in formal French writing and, whatever you
do, don't mention the Corn Laws! Soon, world domination (or
at least a halfway decent job in local government) will be ours.

ENERGY

You need it – they've got it.

ENJOYING IT

Soon after having a baby, when you bump into neighbours or
chat to relatives, they will quite possibly ask you whether you
are enjoying it. What an odd question. Having a new baby is
exhausting and bewildering and repetitive, occasionally
euphoric, but enjoyable?

So to help those neighbours and relatives, we have compiled
a list of more appropriate questions to ask someone recently
delivered of a child:

Are you still experiencing pain when sitting down?
Did your hands shake when you changed the first nappy?

Do you fear the night?

Are you tyrannised by parenting books?

Do you see danger everywhere?

How do you feel about stairs now?

Were you terrified of doing your first poo after labour?

Are you wondering when life will go back to 'normal'?
(*See*, New Normal)

Are you replaying the labour over and over in your
mind?

Do you now cry uncontrollably over any news stories, bad
or good, concerning children?

Have you rung NHS direct yet?

ENTITLEMENT

Your child is entitled to respect, yes; love, certainly; and security, undoubtedly. A daily Calippo and a CBeebies magazine, as well, apparently.

The rise of a child-centred society together with the unprecedented growth of consumerism in recent years seems to have engendered a culture of entitlement amongst our children. With the attitude of Oliver Twist, but a tad less polite, they no longer just *want* more, but damn well expect it, and demand that you give it to them pronto. Or they'll scream.

From material goods to having fun, they know what they want, and it usually involves you getting your purse out. Suggest a family trip to the park or a spot of painting on a Saturday afternoon and she'll look at you with a contemptuous sneer. Three hours of soft play and a trolley dash round Toys R Us is more what she had in mind. It's not just the *amount* of stuff that they want, either. It's got to be the *right* stuff, too. Whilst it may be iced ambrosia for a two-year-old, a Mini Milk is about as appealing as a frozen turd to a brand-savvy five-year-old. And you can forget the idea of buying those small cars in the blue box with the flame on that are half the price of Hot Wheels. His consumerist heart will break on Christmas Day.

As our children speed-rip their way through mountains of birthday presents, tossing the contents aside and pausing only to point out to a doting grandparent that, doh, they've already got one of those, we find ourselves reminding them how enormously privileged they are. We tell them about people in the developing world and those living below the poverty line. And then we get down to the real nitty-gritty – telling them how it was 'in our day'.

Ah yes, the austere seventies. Era of brown tanktops and the Winter of Discontent. Never mind only having an hour on your Wii, we tell them, in our day we were lucky to play Ludo by the light of a candle whilst our bins overflowed in the streets. *And* there wasn't any toast. Think yourself lucky, we say, as we drag them crying from the soft-play place. Play was *never* soft in our day. Concrete surfaces here, asbestos pipes there, but we managed to have fun (and a few life-threatening accidents), oh yes. On Sunday lunchtime, when they hysterically beg not to have to go to Pizza Express *again*, we describe how, in our day, we were lucky to get an annual visit to the Berni Inn for a slice of gammon and pineapple and a clip round the ear for talking at the table. And when it comes to their latest Christmas present haul, don't get us started. Would you like us to spell out the relative merits of an XBox and a Mr Potato Head? *Would* you?

But what good does it do comparing their Nike trainers with our Startrite sandals, their villa holiday in the Med with our wet weekend in a B&B in Tenby? They don't understand the difference any more than we understood when our parents harped on about being locked in the coal bunker for minor misdemeanours, or only getting a clementine and two walnuts in their Christmas stocking. The world has moved on. And we can't blame kids for being brought up in a consumer society gone potty. We, the hard-done-by children of the seventies have wholeheartedly embraced the material world with open hands and numerous credit cards. We've indulged ourselves and our children, so we must reap what we've sown. Once we start on the spending spiral, there's no going back. Better go and buy that Lotto ticket, or take out that loan. Today's Mini Milk is tomorrow's Mini Cooper.

EVENINGS STARTING AT 9 P.M.

That's quite late. By the time they've gone down at 7.30 – oh, let's face it, nearer to 7.45 – and you've swept the plastic kiddie stuff into the corners of the living room, so it's not in your line of vision while watching *Property Ladder*, then made dinner, eaten it, rung your mum, hung the washing up (meant to do that earlier, didn't get time, must have dry pants in the morning), unloaded the dishwasher – Shit! Missed *Property Ladder* – reloaded it and popped to the corner shop for more milk, it's late. If you're sensible you will go to bed at 10 p.m., too. So that's one hour of free time. One solitary hour. Oh . . . Sod.

EXPRESSING: An Opinion

One mother's Electric Breast Pump is another's Foghorn of Sausage-Nippled Misery. Discuss.

F f

FAT

Does your bum look big in this? Yes, of course it does.

FILM-WATCHING WITH THE UNDER FIVES

Apart from that time you misguidedly went to see *Rambo* III
with a spotty-faced lech in 1988, cinema-going has never
been such a challenging experience. After two hours of
unrelenting Paxman-type interrogation about the plot and
three toilet breaks, neither of you has the faintest idea what's
going on.

But *why* is the penguin singing like Elvis, Mummy?
Why indeed.

FINISHING OFF KIDS' FOOD

Since when did half a cold fishfinger and a spoonful of Petit Filous become so tempting?

FISSURES

That's tears in your lady regions, caused by childbirth. Anal fissures are also common in women after childbirth. At least, that's what I read on Wikipedia. I wouldn't know.

FLEXIBLE WORKING

Employers are very keen on the working bit, not so much on the flexible bit. In reality, it's the chance to do five days' work in four days for four days' pay.

FOLDING

A crisis manoeuvre that theoretically allows you to insert a rigid, frothing child into a buggy. Really requires the extra leverage of a well-placed parental knee to pull it off successfully. Complicating factor: buggy on hill. Potential hazards: public humiliation, arrest.

FORMER LIVES

Most of the world arranges its history according to whether things happened before or after a birth. All right, it happens to be the birth of Christ, which was, obviously, a bit of a big deal. You will come to do the same – arranging your personal history either side of a birth, too. There will be Now and there will be BC, with BC in your case standing for Before Children (although it might as well stand for Before Christ, since so many kids think they're the Messiah anyway). In your personal history, BC was a heady era of lock-ins, lazy hangovers and weekends off. It was also a time of industry, when you reached for your career goals, unfettered by the need to relieve the childminder at 4 p.m. and pick up some Calpol on the way home. And you can't quite let BC go. You are as romantically linked to your former life as you are to your first love. Never completely get over it, do you? And how can you, when you have such rich historical archives at your fingertips: the pre-pregnancy clothes you're still waiting to squeeze into, an old diary from three years ago and the many photos of your BC self: on the beach in a bikini (God, such a flat stomach and you didn't even realise!), at parties, weddings, doing up a new home, mooching along the Seine, trekking the Himalayas . . .

There is also plenty of living history, too, since the towns and cities of your former life are packed with bricks-and-mortar reminders of where your past unfurled. It means you can do the equivalent of a London walk on your former self, and what better companion for this trip down memory lane than your child? He can be the attentive tourist to your over-informed tour guide. It will help him understand the real you, get to grips with the reality that the world did exist before he made his entrance into it, and that Mummy used to do 'other stuff', stuff that did not involve CBeebies, Lego or Calpol.

So you know you shouldn't do it, but you drag your child back in time. Wandering through quiet streets or riding atop a London bus, you excitedly point out landmarks from your former life. 'Look, that's the office where Mummy used to work! Huh, the lifts were always breaking down!' Then, 'That pub was where we'd go after work on Fridays and, once, I was sick in the side alley after too much Grolsch on an empty stomach.' You can point out the flats you rented, the restaurants you went to, where there used to be a good curry house but now it's an internet café, and explain how you would usually catch the 171 bus home, but some days would cycle recklessly round Elephant & Castle roundabout instead. Here, yes, here. Looks pretty scary, doesn't it, kiddo? Well it was, but that was me then: fearless, invincible, *young!*

You can talk about how slim you were, how big your office was or how packed your social life. And will your child look at you in wonder? Will he marvel at your wealth of life experience? Will he ask eager questions about what it was like, *really* like, to give a Power Point presentation to ten senior staff members at a conference in Leicester? Will he bugger. He will yawn, or fiddle with his zip, or tell you to stop talking about 'the olden days'.

And he's right. It might as well be Medieval England for all he cares, it's so long ago. Give it up. It's over, I tell you, over! 'Those were the days, my friend, we thought they'd never end, we'd sing and dance forever and a day.' But then we had kids, and all that singing and dancing abruptly stopped. If only we could stop thinking about it, too . . .

FRIENDS
Chapter 6 – Effects of Family Life Upon Female Interaction (Social)

Research was undertaken into the lifestyles of two groups of women: those in their late twenties without children and those in their late thirties with children. The women's relationships with other people were catalogued and analysed to ascertain where they drew their friends from. Dramatic differences were revealed in the number and type of people the different groups of women were mixing with. From this we may draw interesting conclusions about the influence of children upon a woman's social life and social mobility.

Fig 1: Analysis of friendship demographic pre childbirth

Friends from work
Friends from school
Friends from university/higher education
Friends of friends
Foreign friends
Friends of the family
Gay friends
Old friends
Old gay friends
Gay old friends

Fig 2: Analysis of Friendship demographic post childbirth

Other mums, aged between 31 and 43

FUTURE

Before kids, your future was up for grabs. You might live abroad, write that novel or have a rude affair with a saucy young man. Anything could happen, even though it probably wouldn't.

After kids, it's set in stone. It's what you're doing now, times eighteen more years. The End.

G g

GENES

Well, quite frankly, this is a major worry, assuming you are producing a child in the bog-standard his-sperm-meets-your-egg type of way. You get over the initial shock/horror/elation of finding out you are pregnant, only to come to the terrifying realisation that your unborn baby will not, in fact, be an angel-child sent by the Lord, but will be a collection of cells made up of 50 per cent of your genes and, more horrifically, 50 per cent of your partner's.

Dad's dyslexia and long second toes? Your chronic shyness and issues with rage? Whoops – you've just passed them on.

GIVING IN

No, no, no. I said no. Whining won't help, so no. No. No. OH, ALL RIGHT THEN!

Apparently, you should let children win some battles. It helps their self-esteem, but even with this nugget of psychology on your side, there's still something about standing up to a child, only to subsequently crumble under a relentless assault of juvenile whingeing that makes you feel hollow on the inside. And rather pointless. But then, of course, when you do stand firm and win, you feel like you've crushed their tiny, fledgling souls, and that's a dreadfully empty victory.

Probably better to give in, really.

But don't give up.

That's different. And a bit more serious.

GOING TO THE SUPERMARKET ALONE BECOMING A TREAT

The dictionary definition of a treat is 'a source of special delight and pleasure', so it's surprising and rather sad that many real-life women who really exist have said that going round a supermarket alone is a treat. They used to chair board meetings, hit deadlines, recruit and manage staff. Now, unused to solitude or personal space, unable to command their time, they find that a solo trip to Asda is the best life has to offer.

They head through the sliding doors in a businesslike frame of mind, reminding themselves to pick up some Baby Bels for their eldest's lunchbox, but then they slow down, becoming seduced by the intimacy of one woman, alone, shopping, alone, in a supermarket, and alone. Just her, those shelves groaning with produce and an empty trolley. They begin to linger over the ingredients list on a microwave lasagne, they coyly caress the still firm, but almost yielding peaches. They dreamily weave up and down the feminine care aisle. They retrace their steps countless times, talk out loud – 'ha ha, silly me, I forgot the ketchup' – and look up, to catch the man at the fish counter smiling gently at them as he fillets a pollock. They look at their watch. Oh, what unexpected joy – still half an hour to go before they need to collect their child from school. I know, they think, a little unsure, blushing slightly at the boldness of their idea, I'll indulge myself. Just this once. I'll visit the electricals aisle. Shiny, shiny toasters, how you glint out at me. From here, it's soft furnishings, and why not, you deserve it, cookware. My that spatula looks good, and at £2.99, it's reasonably priced, too.

GRASS-IS-GREENER SYNDROME

You think, Please not more hours in the park supervising the sandpit and getting cold feet. He thinks, Lucky her – fresh air, the sun on her face, a piping-hot cappuccino.

He thinks, Commuting – hours on a packed train staring into the open mouth of a dozing businessman from Crawley. You think, How splendid – a nice sit-down and a quiet read.

When it comes to business trips, he says, 'Oh, but they are just night after night in faceless hotel rooms.' You say, 'What I wouldn't give for a night in a faceless hotel room. Nir-bloody-vana, mate. And someone cooks your tea.'

He thinks he's missing all the special moments. You *know* he's missing all the melt-downs and didn't-quite-make-it-to-the-loo-in-time mishaps.

You think, Eating sandwiches at a desk uninterrupted with the chance to skim the paper then check your emails sounds rather decadent. He thinks, It's tough not being able to take a lunch break, chained to a desk all day.

To and fro, back and forth. Yeah but, no but, etc., and also and yes . . .

H h

HAVING MORE THAN ONE CHILD

Some people have one child, love it and go on to have another. But lots of people find it really hard. And go on to have another. That is often how having kids works. It's rare to hear anyone say, 'I just love the daily grind of bringing up kids, so I want more and more.' Instead, you don't precisely understand why you want more, but you do. At least you think you do. And you tell yourself it will 'be all right', when actually you're talking about one of life's greatest challenges, and it might not be all right. It might be financially disastrous, emotionally draining, physically exhausting and quite annoying, too.

Other people collude in this. They will tell you that you'll be OK. They will encourage you to have more kids. This isn't a sophisticated pro-life argument, more a vicarious thrilling to the idea of pregnancy and an unreasoned faith that you will find ways to cope because it's all in such a good cause.

If the 'it'll be all right' argument seems too flimsy for your rational mind, there are lots of ways to persuade yourself that having more than one child is A GOOD THING. You might console yourself that, even if you're skint and you're all sharing a bedroom because you can't afford to move, you will be creating rounded individuals. After all, only children are always complete and utter shitheads, whereas kids from larger families are, without exception, terrifically well-balanced and polite.

You have also provided a playmate for the oldest child. Umm, not if they hate each other, you haven't. Which they might. Look at the Mitchell brothers. Or Cain and Abel. Or Derek and George Alderson from Cumbria who, in 2003, vowed never to speak again after they racked up £25,000 in legal fees when a long feud over a scrap of lawn ended up in court. The sillies.

And then there are the ethical issues. Our planet is overburdened. The population of the world is now at 6.6 billion. By the middle of this century, it's estimated to rise to 9.2 billion. That's *got* to mean longer queues at the Post Office.

And will it make you happy? Look on my statistics, ye mighty, and despair! A meta study of relationships after children in the *Journal of Marriage and Family* found that couples with children were generally less happy than non parents. And – deep breath, repeat prescription for Microgynon, please – it also showed that the more children a couple had, the less happy they were likely to be. Oh arse!

78

So what makes us do it? Perhaps we are slaves to our bodies, bullied by our hormones into boarding the reproduction rollercoaster again. Perhaps we fear that society will judge us if we choose to stick at one. Perhaps we are brow-beaten into it by jealous parents of two, who can't bear the fact that we will be £186,500 better off than them in eighteen years' time. Or maybe we're just complacent. A survey a few years ago of 3,000 women in the UK in their twenties and thirties found that four in ten pregnancies are unplanned. Oopsie.

Still, never mind. You know, it'll be all right.

HEALTH VISITOR

It's a lovely title. Have you ever fancied visiting health upon another? Imagine how satisfying that might feel. Very Mother Teresa-ish. Better still, to a baby. A tiny newborn. You could give him the gift of health, simply with a set of scales and a thrive chart.

If you are new to the world of having kids, and ever so slightly freaked out about the role you find yourself in, you will look to your health visitor much as Richard Gere looked at the Dalai Lama, with a mix of awe, love and a deep longing for enlightenment. And while you will want to scream 'help me, help me, I don't know what I'm doing, I don't know!', you won't dare. You'll maybe even put some make-up on before she arrives. And she will happily ignore the pleading in your eyes for some kind of clue to, well, everything. Not just how to change a nappy or get baby to latch on, but on a more profound level. The question of who you are, where you are, what day it is and when will your life ever go back to 'normal'. She will ignore all this, even though she almost certainly sniffs your desperation. But she can't get into all that because she's rushed off her feet today. Very busy. So instead, she will weigh your child, plot his graph, recommened Infacol and then walk away, to her neat life, where there are perhaps no kids, and certainly no babies, and people can walk out of a house without spending thirty minutes packing a bag and fitting in a last feed. And you will wish she could stay, but you know she has to go. Like when Clint Eastwood leaves Meryl Streep at the end of *The Bridges of Madison County*. Only with fewer bridges.

HIDDEN VEG

When we were little, we got told to eat our greens, but we didn't want to eat our greens. We wanted to eat our beiges, and then have pudding. These days, children still don't want to eat their greens, but we know they should, or they will grow up pale and maladjusted. So instead of standing over them with a rolling-pin at meal times we have become expert vegetable concealers. Children no longer need be affronted by the sight of a pile of steaming spinach on their dinner plate, because we'll find a way, with a bit of trickery and a gallon of tomato sauce, to disguise it.

To hide veg well, think of yourself as a drug pusher, with broccoli and carrots your Class As. Your children, unfortunately, are the sniffer-dog spaniels, alert to even the most finely grated courgette, so to 'push' your veg successfully you must conceal this nutritious pulp in a sea of tomato sauce and perhaps some meat, smothered in grated cheese. As they tuck in, you will rub your hands with glee – you have conned those unsuspecting fools into consuming nutritious food. Ha! Not so picky now, eh?

Hidden veg is a hot potato, as it were, in the commercial world of child nutrition, too. Recipes for meals made with hidden veg are strewn through children's cook books. Heinz recently brought out a range of hidden-veg spaghetti hoops and baked beans, while Waitrose has devised a collection of veg disguises: cute edible rice paper outfits that you can slip over a carrot baton or cauliflower floret to encourage your child to eat its five-a-day. They currently have Doctor Who, Cinderella and Makka Pakka outfits, but are planning to introduce more. All right they're not. I made that bit up. But how ace would that be?

HOLIDAYS

Definition: a day or period of time in which one is exempt from work; *specifically*: time marked by a general suspension of work.

HOLIDAYS WITH CHILDREN

Definition: a day or period of time in which parents are compelled to work; *specifically*: time marked by a general suspension of work for everyone sodding else except you.

If it's a rest you're after, you'd do as well to book yourself in for some major abdominal surgery at your local private hospital. Five days in bed, your own TV and someone on hand to help you wipe your bum. Sound tempting?

Holidays are no longer about relaxation, partying, culture or, in fact, you. Holidays are now about masochistically relocating the tedium of parenting for one or two weeks to somewhere where it will be so much more physically challenging, like a campsite; or spiritually demoralising, like Disneyland; or, if you're very lucky, a combination of both, like Whitley Bay Caravan Park. Is two weeks working twice as hard to care for your children in a hostile environment really worth all the money and effort?

Well, maybe it is. You have a few misguided romantic notions about taking your children on holiday. You imagine Italian trattoria owners being charmed by your delightful blonde moppet, whisking her off into the kitchen to feed her spaghetti and squeeze her rosy cheeks while you enjoy a relaxing meal, watching the fireflies. You picture snapshots of your brood, fresh-faced and healthy, happily munching cod and chips on the quay of a charming fishing village, or the family cooperatively engaged in the building of a magnificent sandcastle complex under azure skies. And, of course, it is like this. Sometimes. And then, most of the time, it's not.

But why not? Well, your choices are distinctly limited when it comes to holidaying with your children. You can forget your pre-children vacational preferences for gallery-visiting, alpine trekking or dancing like a loon till five in the morning. Holidays now need to be strategically planned using the strict criteria of economy, logistics and, well, *children*. Firstly, can you afford to go on holiday *at all*? A full-price plane ticket will be required for your two-year-old who will most probably need to be lifted out of his £125 seat immediately after take-off and firmly restrained in a head-lock on your lap for two hours to prevent him from running up and down the aisle screaming. You might be stung by the 100 per cent school-holiday premium and you will have to stump up for multiple hotel rooms, multiple meals and, most galling of all, multiple entertainments. If it rains you might have to go to an attraction (*see* Attractions) or an even more bizarre shrine to commercialism otherwise known as an 'Experience'. At an 'Experience', you can expect to experience something randomly inappropriate, like a mannequin-filled Blitz in the middle of the Cornish countryside. You, as a fully paid-up member of society, will pay around £14 for this privilege. And your little three-year-old who, though very advanced, of course, has not quite progressed to learning about Hitler's policy of Lebensraum, will also have to pay £9. Or rather, you will. You mug.

Then there's the logistics of getting there. How far can you travel without mutiny on a plane with a four-year-old, a two-year-old and a couple of Thomas The Tank Engine books? An hour? So, that's bye-bye Bali, hello Belgium, then. Can you make it from Kent to Devon with a ten-month-old in a car seat or will you be forced by non-stop screaming into an emergency overnighter at the Travelodge in Swindon? Can you find a decent holiday cottage anywhere within a four-hour driving distance that accepts under-twelves? Can you transport two children, two car seats, a tent, four cases, four duvets, a buggy, a potty, thirty-two nappies, four cuddly toys, six books, a train set and a high chair 150 miles in a Ford Focus? Or will you die trying?

Taking all these factors into consideration, your holiday horizons will probably have to narrow somewhat. Your fortnight in a 3* in Nice might have to turn into four days in a three-berth in Normandy. You'll be living in a space a quarter of the size of your usual accommodation, the children won't go to bed and will wake up early. Your bed will be an unbearably tiny double with a Belgian waffle for a mattress and your mum will be 200 miles away from babysitting duties. You won't know where anything is in the kitchen and there won't be a dishwasher. You will spend a lot of money, visit war cemeteries and argue daily. It will rain. But on the other hand, you'll get a few photos for the family album, you'll be able to go to a French supermarket every day (don't forget your shopping bags!) and eat cheese with impunity. Every holiday cloud has a silver lining. And sometimes it's made of Camembert.

HOLIDAYS WITH GRANDPARENTS

They do a bit to amuse your children, but for this you have to share the same bathroom as your father-in-law.

HOLIDAYS WITH OTHER FAMILIES

The kids will play, the grown-ups will relax, there will be fine wines, feasting, lie-ins. Possibly, all this will happen, but also possibly your kids and their kids have had a little chat and decided to do things differently this year.

HOSPITAL BAG

A vital bit of kit for any expectant mother. Even committed free-birthers might come to their senses when they notice a tiny bottom dangling from their nethers and need to dash off to find someone in a nearby institution who's handy with a scalpel and has a ready supply of anaesthesia. As Baden-Powell once said, '[Bees] are quite a model community for they respect their Queen and kill their unemployed.' Well, that, and some sensible things like 'Be Prepared'. If it's good enough advice for eight-year-old boys with woggles, then it's good enough advice for grown women about to give birth. Gas and air, minor grazing and home six hours later, or five days' bed rest with a healing wound after an emergency C-section? The choice is (very rarely) yours. You'd better get packing.

But what to pack? Well, everything really. There's all the necessary stuff for plugging leaks and easing pain that slightly turns your stomach when you think about it: the industrial-sized maternity pads that will make you look two inches taller when sitting down, the disposable pants, the massive pants, the dark-coloured towels, the dark-coloured oversized T-shirts, the inflatable bottom cushion, the breast pads, the arnica for bruising, Vaseline, Windeze, Gaviscon, Nurofen. Then there are the Babygros, tiny vests, socks, muslins, nappies, cotton wool, blankets, hats, cuddly toys . . . All very valid and possibly useful inclusions. The practical realist in you packs this side of the bag.

If it's your first baby, your inner fantasist might just slip in a few choice items while your realist back is turned. You can't help yourself. You know you're not Victoria Beckham giving birth at the Portland, but you don't see why your birth shouldn't be a pleasurable, nay stylish, experience. So, maybe you will pack that exquisite white lace nightie and silk dressing gown to wear while you are sitting proudly in bed beatifically suckling your newborn. And of course there's room for a mini bottle of Champagne and some good chocolate truffles. And some mules. You haven't actually got any, but you could buy some for the occasion, why the hell not? What about some nice new make-up to put on for your photos? And for when you're in labour, what about some mineral water face spritzers for your birth partner to lovingly mist over your fevered brow. Cartons of drinks, sweets, straws, frozen lollies, Kendal mint cake. The contents of the local homeopath's shelves, a damn good book; oh, and don't forget your iPod loaded with 200 carefully chosen ambient tunes. By the time you've finished, it's as if you've packed in preparation for a major accident at a country house hotel in the Lake District.

But if your birth is anything like mine, you might only get through a bendy straw and ten maternity pads. You might labour in the clothes you arrived in until someone thoughtfully eases you into a breast-flashingly flappy hospital gown. When your partner tentatively approaches you mid-contraction with a spritzer you might hit him and tell him where to squirt his poncey mineral water. You won't be bothered whether Enya's 'Orinoco Flow' is or isn't playing when you go into transition. You will only hear yourself screaming and a midwife telling you to get a grip. And you hate Kendal mint cake anyway. As for beatifically breast-feeding your newborn in white silk whilst quaffing Champagne and nibbling truffles, you might actually be sobbing onto your blood-stained hospital-issue dressing gown as you struggle to get your screaming infant to latch on. Followed by a quick cup of tea and a packet of crisps from the machine in the corridor when they forget to bring you any dinner.

HYPOCRISY IN KIDS

One four-year-old to another: 'You need to share/ You should let me choose which toy to play with because I'm the guest/ Don't say that, it's rude.'

Just listen to yourself, will you?

I i

IF . . . THEN . . .

If you don't . . . then I will . . .
If you do . . . then I won't . . .
 It's the old parenting one-two.

IGNORING YOUR CHILD

Sometimes, when he goes 'watch this, Mum, watch this' I look
over, but I deliberately look about 30 cm to the right of him,
but he thinks I am watching him. Ha!

 Other times, he's going on about some stuff or other and
I'm just chanting in my head, 'Not even listening, not
listening, not, not, not, la la ladi da.' Ha again!

 And thus I survive.

ILLNESS

It's a given – small children with even smaller immune systems get ill. A lot. It doesn't matter whether you are still breast-feeding them at four or force-feeding them organic alfalfa sprouts. They will still succumb. At the very least, effluvia will be running from their noses for about eight months of the year, and come December they will be projectile vomiting into the cracks in your floorboards. They will have the Pox, Slapped Cheek, Hand Foot and Mouth, Scarlet Fever, Croup. It's all very Dickensian, if not a little agricultural. They can't tell you what's wrong, so you speculate wildly. You will look to the internet, but the internet is not your friend. It has a lot of gag-inducing close-up pictures of pustules, and a great many worse-case scenarios for you to stew over, too. Chicken pox causing blindness, that sort of thing. Every two months, you will be pressing a jam jar to their be-speckled skin (*see* Rashes). Three months of your waking life will be spent hanging on the phone to NHS Direct who, after a twenty-minute interrogation, will helpfully advise you to go immediately to your GP. When you get to the GP they will, in turn, helpfully tell you that the cold/cough/fever/vomiting/rash is 'probably' a 'non-specific' virus.

Eventually, after about two years of repeating this fruitless cycle, you learn to panic less and cut out the middle man. You start to favour the do-it-yourself approach. It's true. Calpol and hot Ribena can cure most illnesses known to man. Or at least, children.

Ah, now that's better.

ILLNESS IN PARENTS

When you're a parent, your partner becoming ill is just a big fat inconvenience. You're a man down. It's like he has become ill just to spite you. Gone are the days of tea and sympathy – running to the shops for packets of Nurofen and bottles of Lucozade for your stricken soul-mate; the stroke of the fevered brow; the supportive squeeze of the sweaty hand; the whispered and occasionally even heart-felt commiserations. Now you just want to scream at the inconsiderate bastard that 'IT'S SO NOT FAIR'.

If you are at home looking after a pre-school child, but with a normally modern and equal relationship, a partner's illness can transport you right back to the 1950s. So, you're thinking to yourself, as your blood boils in your veins, apparently, he can feel a bit ill, take a paid sickie, retire to his bed or at the very least to the sofa in front of the TV, and stay there for forty-eight hours. Not only does he not have to go to work, but all his household and childcare duties are relinquished for the dura-tion because there's somebody else around to do them (namely muggins). You, on the other hand, can feel really very ill, get up at 6 a.m., miserably watch your partner disappear down the front path, feed, change, dress and entertain a small child, and then carry on relentlessly doing the same for the rest of the day until you're slumped over the hob at 5 p.m., attempting to stir fry whilst retching into a saucepan. You can't pull a sickie. You can't afford to give in to illness. But he can embrace it with his outstretched fluffy dressing gown. The jammy swine.

Of course, it's not really your partner's fault. As society doesn't see looking after one's children as 'work', being sick for a stay-at-home parent is not practically or financially viable. Plus your kids are the toughest employers. On discovering that you have a stinking cold, they don't say 'Never mind, Mum, I'll sort myself out with some Lego and a film while you take a restorative nap.' They say, 'Ahhh, poor Mummy,' in a sickly, fake voice before jumping on your chest and demanding you build them a den. So you will force yourself to find new levels of mental and physical strength and when your partner returns from work, he will simply assume that if you survived the day, albeit with vomit down your shirt and only crisps for tea, you can't really have been that ill anyway.

IMAGINARY WORLD

It's where I go to for five minutes' break. I'm much younger, with killer clothes, a dazzling smile, no post-pregnancy weight and an absurdly gorgeous boyfriend and we waft about being fabulous. Usually in New York, or Paris. Now then, where was I? Ah yes, fishfingers.

IMPRACTICAL THREATS

Right, do that one more time and you won't be allowed to watch TV all week! Shit, what have I said . . . ?

Sometimes, after asking nicely, then asking not so nicely, then shouting, then getting *reeeeaalllly* angry, impossible threats are all you've got. But they work for no one. They are too extreme. I'll ring your teacher and tell her you're being naughty (like I'm going to draw the school's attention to your crap behaviour); if you don't stop whining for an ice-cream, we're not staying to watch the clowns (oh great, that's £35 and the rest of the evening down the drain); if you don't put your shoes on right now, we're not going to the beach (now we'll be stuck in watching the Spanish version of *Who Wants To Be A Millionaire* and playing Patience on the cold tiled floor).

Always remember, it's the child you're meant to be penalising, not yourself.

INFACOL

Orange-flavoured flob delivered via a pipette. I'd rather have wind. If your baby could talk, she would say the same.

INSTINCT

Let it guide you, says Dr Spock, and do what *you* feel is right. But Dr Spock, my instincts are telling me I'm really confused.

INTENSITY

With children, the highs can be so high, the lows, so very low.

I love you, I love you, I love you. *I hate you, I hate you, I hate you.*

You're so adorable, I could eat you up. *You're so annoying, I'm very close to slapping you.*

Gorgeous angel. *Little bugger.*

Come here for a cuddle. *Get off me, will you? I need some space.*

So proud. *So ashamed.*

All in all, having kids is an intense rollercoaster ride. It plunges up and down, and there's lots of screaming and vomiting involved.

Or perhaps I'm just unbalanced.

INTERRUPTIONS

All those broken conversations, all those unanswered questions. Like Pinter, but with a bit more mental torture.

INVISIBILITY

Remember when you used to turn heads just sauntering down the road? Try doing that with a buggy. Hey presto, you have completely disappeared.

J j

JOLLY PHONICS

Y-ou m-u-s-t be b-l-oo-d-y j-o-k-ing. L-i-st-en-ing to th-e-m t-a-k-ing h-a-l-f an h-ou-r to s-ou-n-d ou-t a s-en-t-en-ce is a-b-ou-t as j-o-ll-y as v-i-s-i-t-ing D-u-s-t-i-n H-o-ff-m-a-n's d-e-n-t-i-s-t.

JUDGING

Once you become a mother, marching up to the moral high ground and sticking your flag in it becomes something of a daily ritual. We just can't help ourselves. When I was a Marketing Manager for a small publishing house and she was a Technical Director for a travel company, we couldn't judge each other because we hadn't a clue what each other actually did every day. Computers, blah, html, blah, targets, yawn, year-on-year blahs, profit margins, blah-de-dullsville-arizona-blah. That sort of thing. We didn't understand each other's jobs and we certainly weren't interested. Her skirts might have been indecorously short on occasion, but what of it? Live and let live, that's what I say.

Or at least, that's what I *used* to say. Now we've popped a few sprogs and signed up for the same job description, we just can't keep our opinions to ourselves. And we're so very interested in the minutiae of each other's child-rearing practices. My idea of a healthy fruit drink is her idea of serious dental abuse. I see the television as a harmless relaxing leisure activity. She sees it as the monstrous corruption of impressionable young minds.

Fine. Whatever. But she lets her baby wear socks!

And it's not just other mothers giving you the benefit of their wisdom, either. Take those first tentative steps into town with your newborn and the world and his wife will be queuing up to tell you where you're going wrong. 'It's winter – she should be wearing gloves! It's summer – why isn't he wearing a hat? You shouldn't breast-feed in a restaurant – you wanton exhibitionist!' You're usually so mortified that you scuttle off shame-facedly having failed to answer the busy-bodies back. You smart indignantly, endlessly replaying the conversations in your mind. 'Well, she was wearing gloves, you interfering loon, but she took them off! Yes he was wearing a hat, you doddering fool, but he threw it in the pond! Why ever not breast-feed in a restaurant, you anachronistic old goat? We were having our lunch, not pole dancing!'

You think they should just mind their own flaming business. Minding *your* own business, however, is a very different matter.

Socks, you say? Yes, very cute I'm sure. But you *do* know they can stunt your baby's growth??

JUGGLING

You thought you were busy when you just had the responsibilities of a home and a job. Then you add children into the equation and quickly discover that they need round-the-clock attention. This basically means you now have too much to do, or at least, no time to do some of it. The non-child-related stuff, usually. It is staggering how you can spend an entire day with a child, setting yourself only one objective outside of caring for him or her – make hair appointment, for example – and you actually will not achieve this.

The physical juggling of rushing hither and thither, shunting a buggy, carrying a toddler, picking up this, sorting out that is exhausting, but it's the mental juggling that can really cripple you. Before children, your brain – beyond thoughts relating to work – was roughly given over to 15 per cent domestic affairs, 10 per cent planning next holiday, 10 per cent Pinot Grigio or Sancerre?, 10 per cent relationships, 10 per cent culture, 8 per cent empty thoughts, 2 per cent should ring Mum, 30 per cent where to go tonight, 5 per cent buy or rent. Then you have children and your brain space is divided up with 10 per cent book-bag, 60 per cent mundane child-related domestic hokum, 5 per cent escape fantasies, 15 per cent beer or wine, 5 per cent remorse over beer or wine, 5 per cent confused thoughts.

Of course, we don't make life easy for ourselves when it comes to juggling. The need to juggle is quickly followed by anxiety about juggling in the right manner. I can't play with you now because I'm cooking you a nutritious dinner, but maybe I should be playing with you instead. I don't know. Which is more important? The result can be a sense of life perpetually slipping from your grasp, like wrestling a greasy piglet. Between the house, kids, school, work, planning the weekends, doing the shopping, keeping up with friends, you are never quite on top of anything. You will never pin it all down, or get to the end of your To Do list without another six things creeping in at the top. Something has to give. You will have to drop your standards and change your ideals. Your job is now not to complete the To Do list, but to placidly accept that you never can.

The only good news is that juggling as a parent, like juggling as a juggler, can be learned; mastered even. Stay hydrated, eat well, get to bed early and you can juggle with the best of them. The only difference is that professional jugglers probably get time off from juggling. Unless, of course, they are parents, too.

Imagine that? You thought you had it bad . . .

JUICE

It's not something we adults get all that worked up about, but it plays a gargantuan role in a young child's life. They are OBSESSED with it. What is *in* that stuff?

K k

KICKING OFF

It's what kids do. And what you do when they do what they do.

KIDS AS:

Omnipresent malignant forces: you're out for a drink with mates, but not drinking too much because you know he's making a mental note to wake up especially early. You break your ankle slipping on a Power Ranger 'accidentally' left on the stairs. And what's that strange birthmark on the back of his head, anyway?

Conduits of truth: 'Granny, what is an interfering harridan? Daddy says you are one.'

* * *

Experimental scientists: 'If I cut off the cat's whiskers, will he fall over?' 'If I smash the TV screen with my hammer, can Bob the Builder climb out?'

Unsettable alarm clocks: they go off at 6.30 a.m. every day, but sometimes throw in a 4.05 just to keep you guessing.

Global-branding executives: 'My favourite song is "Living in a Cheerios World", Mummy.' Christ! Can't Madonna enunciate any better? Or is this one branded breakfast cereal too far?

Budding linguists: 'Mummy, can I 'ave a happle.' She's the charming Eliza Doolittle to your exasperated Henry Higgins.

Purveyors of wisdom: 'Mummy, wind is pollution and the polar ice-creams are melting. It's true.'

Able spoonerists: From the par cark to the kool tit he wants for Christmas, he's an unsuspecting craster of the maft.

Lousy swearers: 'Fucky 'ell, you big dog poof.'

Incisive TV critics: 'Mum – this EastEnders thing is reeeallllly boooooring!'

All mouth and no trousers thrill-seekers: stop the ride, he wants to get off.

KIDS' PARTIES

From now on, it's your kids who go to parties, not you.

Mind you, apart from the lack of shagging and fag burns on the carpet, there are some startling similarities: a lot of noise, mess, spillages, vomit on the sofa, a fight, someone getting locked in the toilet, a couple of minor head injuries, a broken coffee table, girls sobbing on the stairs. What's worse is that this carnage is taking place at 1.30 on a Sunday afternoon. And it's at *your* place.

Yes, if you fancy spending loads of cash in order to get supremely anxious while unintentionally showcasing your normally well-behaved child as a hysterical spoiled brat, then hosting an under five's birthday party is the way forward. Here's how it works:

1. Get stressed searching desperately for venue. Realise ten days is too short notice and that proper mums and organised dads have pre-booked their children's parties six months in advance. Experience feelings of guilt and inadequacy and resort to having it at home.
2. Get stressed sorting out guest list. Worry that your child has no real friends as his only conversational skills involve saying 'poobumfart' repeatedly and 'mine's better than yours'. Decide to invite whole nursery class so at least a handful will turn up and no one will get offended.
3. Panic as whole class bar two who are on holiday

respond in the affirmative. You didn't realise that kids will do anything for some jelly and a party bag. Doh.

4. Panic as realise thirty children will be descending on your small, newly decorated, terraced house.

5. Get stressed about party bags. Worry about engaging in rampant consumerism and buying numerous small plastic items which have been toxically manufactured and flown in from China for British children to play with for forty-five seconds then discard. Consider that parents would approve and think you green and righteous if you bought a packet of cress seeds for each child as alternative. Decide that children would riot if given a packet of cress seeds as alternative. Buy toxic Chinese plastic items instead, but put in recycled paper bags as exercise in political-correctness damage limitation.

6. Get stressed about birthday cake. Search supermarkets in vain for cake decorated in rather niche theme of 'shark attack' son has chosen. Decide to make cake instead. Spend five sleepless nights worrying about making cake in shape of shark jaws and severed leg when have only ever made chocolate rice-crispy cakes. Decide to pay someone else too much money to make cake at short notice.

7. Get stressed about party food. Worry about serving sugar- salt- and fat-filled crap to other people's children. Consider parents would approve and think you

respectable and righteous if you served hummus and wholemeal pitta, crudités and fruit kebabs. Decide that children would riot if served vegetable matter at a party. Buy cheap sausage rolls, crisps and Jammy Dodgers instead, but make a salad as a consolatory green table decoration.

8. Think about getting party entertainer. Think again when find out price. Ask partner to improvise by making a few balloon animals and getting his old Emu down from the loft.

9. Spend several evenings in consumerist denial on hands and knees in production line with partner and next-door neighbour making up thirty toxic Chinese party bags.

10. Spend party morning bracing yourself. Afternoon comes and host fantastic children's party with a permanent smile and clenched teeth. Other children have lots of fun tearing through house and stamping Quavers into cracks in your floorboards. Own child embarrasses by asking each guest where his present is and tantruming when he doesn't win Pass the Parcel. Two children require plasters. One child cries. Take forty-seven photos of own child blowing out candles on superb £60 shark attack cake. Open wine. Drink wine and eat crisps with other parents. Notice that Emu is going down fairly well, though also consider that you don't really care any more.

11. Other children leave, whooping with consumerist

glee when they open party bags. Feel vindicated. Assess state of house as surprisingly OK except for muddy footprints on floorboards and one turd left in toilet bowl. Own child spends next seven hours opening presents which fill you with First World guilt and shame and which you know will not fit into your small terraced house.

12. Feel relieved that it is 364 days before you will have to host party again. Finish wine. Feed rocket, radicchio and baby leaf salad to rabbit. Happy Birthday, Flopsy.

KILLING TIME

If a child rises at approximately 6.30 a.m. and goes to bed at approximately 7 p.m., then that makes twelve and a half hours in which it is awake, and for almost all of that time it will not be able to amuse itself. You'll have to do it. What are you going to do? You're going to fill the day with scheduled activities, and for each one you will have an approximate duration in your head. Go to the park – should occupy an hour and a half. Pop to shops = roughly forty-five minutes. Lunch = thirty minutes. You are essentially counting down to their bedtime. After bedtime, you return to the adult world, where time flies and can be easily filled, rather than the childish world, where time must be painstakingly portioned off lest everybody drift perilously into a no man's land of unstructured hell where anything could happen, none of it good.

Look at the faces of the parents at your local soft-play place.

Bored. They're thinking, This is brain-puréeingly tedious for me, but he's enjoying it and if I can just stick it here until 12 p.m., then that's the morning sorted. THE MORNING SORTED! Jesus buggering Christ, how depressing. They're not thinking, I want to remain here until 12 p.m. because then that will have been an enjoyable and rewarding use of our morning, for both of us. No. It's just, phew, that's the first landmark chunk of the day dispatched, now, how are we going to get through the afternoon . . . ?

Of course, sometimes even the most clock-conscious parent can enjoy the moment for what it is. Even if it is Wriggle 'N' Rhyme at the library. But more often than not they are just there for something to do, because there's still another four hours until bedtime and junior isn't going to fill it by sitting down and reading the papers like a sensible adult would. You've got to wait another eighteen years for that. Best just to focus on bedtime, now currently three hours and fifty-nine minutes away. And counting . . .

L l

LACK . . .

. . . of self-confidence, money, work, freedom, spare time, time alone, romance, etc., etc.

LEAKAGE

You probably never leaked before you gave birth. You may have seeped a bit. That's OK. Mild seepage is acceptable. Full-scale leakage is not. After childbirth you will leak. Really leak. Like you have been run over by an upside down hedgehog – hold you up and fountains of liquid will spurt extravagantly from any and every orifice.

You were told that you would bleed after a baby, but dear me, the quantity of blood that will escape you. It's a gore-fest on your Kotex. You start to wonder, is it OK to be losing so much blood? When does lochia stop being lochia and start being a haemorrhage?

You've bought some breast pads, too, because you read that milk can leak from your breasts between feeds. This is correct. It can also stream from them, drenching a breast pad faster than you can say 'let-down reflex'. Which can be quite a let-down. Especially if you've just put on a clean shirt.

If your pelvic floor is shot. Hang on, what do I mean if? *Because* your pelvic floor is shot, you may pee yourself sporadically, and, in addition, yo-yoing hormones and sleep deprivation will play havoc with your emotions, too, so you'll be crying over anything, from Sudanese famine to running out of jam.

To top this all off, your hair falls out, too. Oh my God, not my hair. This is too much. This isn't leakage, this is a mass exodus. Everything is leaving my body. It started with the baby, and now my hair, my milk, my blood, my very life force. This is like dying. My body has become a one-way street and everything's off! Stop me up, please. I need a bung and some tight bandages. I need a Lycra catsuit. Where's the boy who stuck his thumb in the dyke when you want him?

LETTING YOURSELF GO

You didn't let it go. It just buggered off while your back was turned.

LEXICON

When you become a parent your vocabulary alters. There are lots of words you haven't used since you were a child, plus you can no longer call a spade a spade. These are our current favourites:

Bodily Parts and Functions

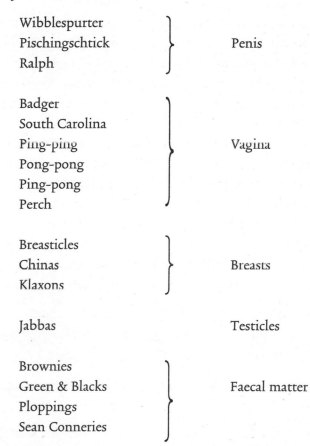

Wibblespurter
Pischingschtick   } Penis
Ralph

Badger
South Carolina
Ping-ping   } Vagina
Pong-pong
Ping-pong
Perch

Breasticles
Chinas   } Breasts
Klaxons

Jabbas   Testicles

Brownies
Green & Blacks   } Faecal matter
Ploppings
Sean Conneries

111

Gush
PP   } Urine
Sprinklings
Diggle

Parmps
Guffs
Fluffs   } Farts
Squeets
Knicker-shakers

Rummers
Flurns   } Burps

Gip
Barfchester Chronicles } Vomit

Taking the bus to Barfchester   Vomiting

Scouting for pearls
Green fingering   } Nose picking
Snot larking

Honkus ponkus
Glurty   } Describing
Nongy nongy   anything repellent

And from the parental pantry

Numpties	Food
Fishy dishy	Cod mornay
Nicey ricey	Risotto
Hot rocks	Roast potatoes
Pot o' flob	Yogurt
Pig in a pokey	Sausage roll
Skiddy cake	Pain au chocolat
Titty biscuits	Cherry Bakewells
Gribbles	Healthy snacks
Shibbles	Unhealthy snacks
Rolf & Chesney	Sausage & chips
Eggy bread	French toast
Smeggy bread	Nutella on toast

LIBERAL DISCIPLINING

Fortunately, walloping one's child with a slipper and locking them in the cellar for burping at the dinner table is somewhat frowned upon these days. Not actually illegal unless you leave a big footprint on their bottoms and point it out to a nearby copper, of course, but very definitely frowned upon by most reasonable members of society.

This is good news for our kids, obviously, and hopefully for society in general. It does, however, leave us with the vexing issue of how to discipline our kids in the twenty-first century. Physically terrorising them was the cop-out option for previous generations. Fear rendered fifties' kids instantly compliant (if a little jumpy and depressed). Perfect table manners and the brass polished without so much as a whinge or groan. It seems that today's parents are going to have to put in a lot more time and effort to achieve the same impressive results humanely. (There's always shouting, of course, but even that's about as Zeitgeisty as sending kids up chimneys.)

And so we have moved towards liberal disciplining, which basically means not telling your children off very much. It involves a lot more listening *to* and a bit less talking *at*. It's *liberal* because it's positive and reasonable. But mainly, of course, because it's so difficult to discipline positively and reasonably that you end up letting most things go. Won't get dressed in the morning? Ah well, we'll just be late for school then. Brattishly demanding an ice-cream at the park? Ah well, she says, reaching for her purse, I suppose it's only a pound. Proponents of liberal disciplining advise us to *choose our battles*. The only problem with that is that it often seems easier to choose to have no battles at all. When it comes down to it, pretty much nothing seems worth suffering the inconvenience and indignity of a full-blown hissy-fit. Instead, 'Oh, I'll just do it then, shall I?' will become your mantra.

If we do want to make a concerted effort to be slightly more *constructively* liberal, we can have a go at *positive parenting*. This, we are told, is the best way to bring up considerate, happy, well-adjusted individuals. And who wouldn't want to do that? It's all about modelling reasonable behaviour, using positive language and giving attention and praise for good behaviour whilst ignoring or distracting from bad. Of course, it's easy to remain calm at all times if you have been lobotomised. Harder if you have not. For example, modelling good behaviour means being nice and polite to your partner in front of your child, which is difficult when the lazy bastard toe-rag has failed to empty the dishwasher again. I don't instinctively want to hug my precious offspring and calmly say 'it's OK, darling, I know it was an accident and understand that you're feeling a little defensive and embarrassed, but Mummy is a little bit sad right now' when they have just hit me on the head with a plastic cricket bat. I want to shout 'OWWWW! THAT BLOODY HURT! YOU CLUMSY IDIOT!', and flounce off in a big strop. What positive way is there of telling a child 'JESUS CHRIST! NOOO! DO NOT RUN INTO THE ROAD!'? I'm afraid 'Would you mind terribly staying on the pavement please, sweetheart?' doesn't really cut it.

So whilst it's certainly something to aspire to, positive parenting is often more of an ideal than a reality. In practical terms, liberal disciplining frequently needs the back-up of the twin big guns of child control – bribery and blackmail. Where counting to three, being nice and pointing out imaginary squirrels has failed, a Milky Way and few well-placed threats to dob them in to Father Christmas or the Easter Bunny might just do the trick.

LINUS

Be it a scuzzy rag or Mum's left eyebrow, most kids have a wucky (that's a comfort item or security blanket, to you and me).

LISTENING

It's like a horror film. You're having a bit of a barney with your partner and suddenly you pause. Stand stock still. Your skin prickles with goose bumps and you think, shuddering, We are no longer alone, are we? There is someone standing behind me, isn't there? You turn slowly round. It's . . . your child. Listening.

Having a child is more than simply no longer being a couple. It is acquiring a witness to your relationship. He has infiltrated your twosome like Donnie Brasco in the New York mafia and he's clocking everything: the good, the bad and the shoddy. When you fought before, no one knew (except maybe the neighbours). Now small people – and I don't mean passing midgets – observe your rows. In fact, they observe all the colours on your relationship spectrum: the casual rudeness, the wounded atmospheres, the rejected advances. It's like installing CCTV in every room and running it past a trainee therapist. You are not you-two any more, warts and all, you are publicly accountable.

Children can't keep it to themselves, either. They will dish up all those crappy scraps of everyday life to the nearest available listener, instinctively understanding that they have mileage as anecdotes. Mum pees in the shower. She picks her nose while driving. Dad never washes his hands after a wee. Yeah, go on, kids, tell your friends, tell Auntie Jane, tell Meryl at nursery, tell the bloody local paper. Have a good old laugh, all of you: laugh it up.

They clock all your truly sub-standard parenting moments, too, and will simply burst to tell someone about those priceless gems. Like the time Mummy fell down the stairs and banged baby's head against the wall. That was a cracking yarn for Granny. Or that ding-dong Mum and Dad had over who's packing the book-bag. That filled a pause round the dinner table at a mate's place. Most toe-curling of all is the public naming and shaming that is News Time at school, when your dob-happy offspring will be invited to share a titbit of family life with his classmates. Some children keep it simple – 'we went to a farm' – while others rabbit on like Ronnie bleedin' Corbett, airing vast armfuls of dirty family laundry in the process: '. . . and then he had to have all his stitches out, and there were thirty-two . . .'

So from now on you need to be on your best behaviour. You are the school, they are the Ofsted inspectors. You are the teenage shop-lifter, they are your electronic tag. They are the pimps and you are, oh dear me yes, most definitely their bitches.

LONELINESS

Loneliness is a crowded room. Or it was back in my working days when I found myself stranded awkwardly by the goat's cheese canapés at the annual sales conference in a hotel on the ring road in Basingstoke. Once I had a small baby, however, work dos seemed to be positively taunting me with the lure of social opportunity. Motherhood had become the new Basingstoke. *This* was *real* loneliness. Witness:

- Coping during the day without help from partner who had returned to work after blink of eyelid, otherwise known as paternity leave.
- Coping without help from close family having told mother at age eighteen would rather do something unpleasant with hot pins than live near her.
- Not speaking for seven hours due to self-consciousness at novice attempts at baby-talk with unresponsive infant.
- Being awake at 3.41 a.m. for eighteenth consecutive night while partner peacefully slumbers in spare room.
- Being unable to leave house for fear of a) baby crying in public place, b) baby pooing in public place, c) baby needing feeding in public place, d) baby falling asleep outside nap time, e) baby waking up *inside* nap time, f) *self* crying in public place.
- Being unable to leave house due to not having had shower or brushed hair for five days.
- Being unable to leave house due to having lost a) purse and b) keys.
- Being unable to go anywhere on public transport due to not being able to collapse buggy without handing baby to random stranger.
- Being unable to go anywhere in car due to sustained incompetence at fitting car seat.
- Being unable to go anywhere on foot due to worrying about negotiating doors/steps/roads with buggy.
- Not being in NCT group.

- Being in NCT group where no other mum had baby who cried all time and had head shaped like frying pan.
- Being unable to go to gay friend's all-nite club-fest thirtieth birthday party.
- Expressing.
- Expressing.
- Expressing.

No, there were no two ways about it. New motherhood was a solitary old business – exacerbated by shock, awe and the comparisons with my oh-so-recent sociable pre-child existence that my brain kept annoyingly making. But it did get better. Soon my baby began to smile, and then to laugh at my jokes! Wow, this was better than adult interaction! It wasn't so lonely now. A little insular perhaps – a lot of one-on-one peekaboo action and not much intelligent conversation. But not lonely. My new best mate and I started to feel confident enough in each other's company to venture out. We thought we could take on the world. Well, a mother and toddler group anyway. We walked in to the throng. He crawled off to the toy cooker. I found myself stranded awkwardly by the custard creams. A nauseating feeling overwhelmed me. Oh. God. Crowded rooms, Basingstoke, noOOO! . . .

LOOKING FORWARD TO . . .

. . . anything, when kids are involved, is the triumph of hope over experience. Again and again we create scenes of serenity, sunshine and ease in our heads as we plan the forthcoming day, only to have our children scythe through them like Vikings through a Celtic village. Just by being small and clumsy and not yet able to master their emotions, children have the ability to not exactly mess things up, but to certainly nudge them towards the brink of chaos. They can transform even the simplest, most common of activities, like going to a café, into a scruffy, piecemeal experience, often involving raised voices, soiled undergarments and mild peril.

One is reminded of Thatcher's speech on winning the 1979 election. 'Where this is discord, may we bring harmony...' Children prefer the opposite. 'Where there is harmony, may we bring discord; where there are no tissues, may we bring a gigantic snotty sneeze; where there is a quiet café, may we bring a spilling of drinks; where there is no toilet, may we bring the need to go to the toilet urgently; and where there is hope, may we bring despair.'

So if you ever catch yourself looking forward to a forth-coming family event with a soupçon of enthusiasm, stop it at once. Really, you should know better.

(*See also* Magical moments that just aren't.)

M m

MAGICAL MOMENTS THAT JUST AREN'T

We are fed images of magical family moments from way before we even consider having children. There are certain points in the calendar, certain key events in a child's life, certain intimate moments in the day that are romanticised in our collective psyche. These are what we are implicity signing up for when we bin the contraception, but they are idealised snapshots of family life, and for that reason, highly unreliable. Christmas, bedtime stories, breast-feeding, family mealtimes, holidays, country walks. You can picture them all as magical, but the reality is often far from . . .

There are so many magical moments that just aren't, that having children would seem to be a giant exercise in shattering dreams. The only thing that makes up for it is that there are also some magical moments that *are*, it's just that we never expected them to be. I once took my kids to the launderette when my washing machine was bust and, much to my surprise, had a perfectly splendid half-hour with them, observing other people's knickers looping by, opening tumble dryers, watching spin-cycle lights going on and off. It would have been tedious on my own; with them it was fun. So don't despair when your four-year-old turns Easter into a chocolate egg smash-and-grab raid then vomits on your mother-in-law's sofa, because, unsuspected by you, Tuesday week might turn out to be quite, quite marvellous.

MEALTIMES

I don't know how they do it on the continent, all those cute Italian kids sitting round the family table independently hoovering up spaghetti. All around, the buzz of interested chatter and the ripple of laughter. A cork being lovingly eased from a bottle of full-bodied Chianti. The breaking of bread; a grandparent's benevolent smile. Empty plates. Full stomachs. Happy families.

Ah yes, the stuff of life.

But not your life, unfortunately.

For many parents, children's mealtimes verge more on *Fawlty Towers* than Florentine trattoria. Is that the vague whiff of dread and pessimism emanating from the kitchen, or is it just a cauliflower being boiled to buggery? You've tried your level best, of course. Wanting to feed your children well is such a primal urge. You've hand-rolled organic chicken nuggets and knocked up nutritious pasta sauces whilst unloading the dishwasher and making Daleks out of Play Doh. You've presented courgettes on seventeen separate occasions and then consigned them to the ever-growing list of 'unmentionable' vegetables that must be bought and puréed into sorbet under the cover of darkness. You've roasted, stir-fried, steamed and grilled; cajoled, bribed, bargained and spooned.

But for what? Your kids still groan and writhe at the abhorrent sight of some lightly poached salmon. A tomato-and-lentil bake can actually reduce them to tears. Some nights you think you might as well tip the contents of the saucepan straight into the bin. Or the dog. Cut out the infuriating middle-child and save yourself having to crawl desperately around on your hands and knees with the Dustbuster. Eventually you retreat down the path of least resistance. With kids, familiarity breeds content. You narrow a list of acceptable meals down to four and rotate them, serving everything with broccoli and sweetcorn. No more fancy tricks with a wet haddock for you.

And even if your children are actually eating the food you have so devotedly prepared, either they bolt it like mad dogs or you are faced with a test of nerve-shattering endurance waiting for them to finish it. With the attention span of fleas with ADHD, some children are incapable of concentrating long enough to eat more than two mouthfuls in a row without the coaching of a university boat race cox. COME ON! . . . ONE MORE! . . . AND ANOTHER . . . KEEP IT UP! . . . NEARLY THERE! . . . You just have to sit it out and wait, watching them agitatedly, teeth gritted behind a forced smile, a growl lurking at the back of your throat. You wonder how many times you can watch him drop a piece of broccoli en route to his mouth before you will feel compelled to grab his fork and shove it in for him. You ponder whether he'll be able to identify the useful edge of a knife by the time he goes to university. You contemplate the fact that you could have flown to Paris in the time it's taken him to eat two sausages and a broccoli floret. And whilst reflecting on how strange it is that you're bloody starving and he's evidently not, you pinch a sausage from his plate. And then a potato. You obviously want them: he doesn't. Yes, he'll be finished in no time now. And the whole sorry business will be over for another day.

MEAT

Kids love meat. Especially mince. M is for Mince, mountains of mince . . .

Which is perhaps why a 2008 ad campaign by GoVeg.com and PETA was always going to run into trouble. Its tag was 'feeding kids meat is child abuse'. Well, it's not the kind of child abuse the NSPCC comes across on a daily basis, I'd wager, but their point is meat can make children fat and is often full of crap. Now, you might take that on board and resolve to sort out something appetisingly veg-based for tea, but try breaking this message to your kids. 'Sorry, guys, we're having salad tonight because that pie there is basically child abuse, right?' You'll have a mini revolt on your hands. This is as inflammatory as Marie Antoinette's famously mis-quoted answer to the starved masses, 'Let them eat cake.' Them poor Frenchie peasants wanted their bread as much as our poor British babies want their sausages. Although, of course, if she'd invited my kids to eat cake as an alternative to all other staples, they would have been delighted – they adore cake even more than they adore meat. But I digress. The point is, kids love meat. This preference for animal products over organic matter is obvious in the way a child approaches its meal. It doesn't matter how elegantly arranged the broccoli – 'look, son, little trees!' – or how al dente the carrot sticks, he or she will always go for the meat first. A sausage on the plate renders all other foodstuffs invisible. Sadly, this means that by the time they work their way round to the veg component, it is a cold, floppy, unappetising remnant, sitting pathetically in a pool of its own gravy. Well, of course they don't want to eat it *now*.

This primal love of meaty food must be slightly offensive if you are vegetarian, but as it's so hard to deny a child its fleshy fix, many veggie parents bow to the meat pressure and present it to their salivating offspring. It's just so much easier to slap a bloody great plate of spag bol down in front of them once a week and see them pounce upon it like pigs at a trough. Slurp slurp slurp. Job done. Meaty, mincey, marvellous.

MESS

Children need mess, because it's stimulating, apparently. A tidy house is no good for their developing minds. Ironic, because the exact opposite is true for their mothers.

Children are mess-making machines. Even the not very messy ones. And they do the messing up in so many different ways. Sometimes accidentally, because they're clumsy, or distracted or over-excited. Sometimes to get a laugh, albeit wry. My son likes to smash up a jigsaw once completed and throw the pieces over his shoulder whilst pulling a comedy surprised face. It is quite funny, but also very messy. Sometimes, the mess-making is entirely pointless. I'm thinking of those kids who come round to play, wander into a room, pick up a basket of Lego, upend it then walk out. An act of such wanton point-lessness, it makes slapping oneself about the face with a tea tray look rich with meaning.

Children make mess in many different media, too. There's wet mess, which can be sloshed juice, bath water poured down the wrong side of the shower curtain, spit, snot or wee, any time, any place, any where. Or clothes mess, including shoes shed on entry, pissy pants peeled off and tossed asunder, millions of tiny socks forever drying on the airer, forever slip-ping onto the floor. There's also eating mess, not to be confused with Eton mess, which is a sort of pudding. Although, you know kids, they could get in a right mess eating Eton mess. Plus they mess with your head (see, This Entire Book) so that you find yourself wanting to get messed up and messy on red wine, just to cope with all the bloody mess.

So how to tackle the mess? There's basically no solution. You could try to cordon off sections of your house just so you have some tiny mess-free oasis to retreat to when all the mess starts to mess you up. Some parents don't allow their children into the living room, for example. But before you employ this tactic in your own home, you have to ask yourself two questions:

1. Where else are we going to hang out?
2. Am I a Nazi?

Your children, after all, have a right to your home, too. It's just that they regularly abuse that right by mistaking it for a landfill site.

As a distraction, I compose Dr Seuss style poems about mess. I find it helps. A bit. Here we go . . .

> I have some mess here in my bed,
> I have some mess here in my head.
> I like to roll about in mess,
> I like to wear it as a dress.
> I make a mess, a lake of mess,
> I like to bake a cake of mess.
> I make the best of all my mess,
> My more is less but mess is best.

ME TIME

Before you have children, 'me time' is just plain old time. Having a bath? Reading a book? Nibbling on a bar of Green & Black's whilst watching ER? Sleeping? These 'leisure' activities don't happen in specially designated and labelled contexts. Just bog-standard real time. The concept of 'me time' does not exist. Because you *are* me. All the time. (No, not *me* me, but *you* me.) If you see what I mean. Yeah, maybe you have a partner, but he/she isn't so demanding of your time that you need to aggressively annex some of it for yourself like Her Majesty's Imperial Army marching into Bechuanaland. They are quite happy to be ignored for two hours while you read the Sunday papers and don't persistently hammer on the bathroom door demanding you assemble their Scalextric track when you are busy enjoying yourself with some bath oils and a loofah.

Post children, the concept of special 'me time' begins to materialise. Indeed, as a parent of small children, you devote so much time to them that time spent on your own or pleasing yourself is as elusive and fleeting as a sunny day at Wimbledon. You are constantly on the go, 'doing' for other people. You can guarantee that your child will urgently need the toilet as soon as you've lathered up in the shower and will be incapable of thinking of any game to play with their playdate that doesn't involve you crawling about on all fours or blowing up eighteen balloons. You are so busy being a parent that it feels like you have very little time to just be *you*. And so the time you do have is precious and important. This I understand. But why does it have to be called *me* time?

Because of the appropriation of these parental moments of personal leisure and relaxation by cynical fat-cat ad execs with a new angle on shifting some aspirational toiletries or chocolate bars. Everyone knows that Father's Day is a commercial construct. But what about 'me time'? I mean, when else would you use a £35 scented candle? Obviously it would be no good for a hurried five-minute shower on a normal-time school morning. But it would be ideal to accompany a forty-five-minute soak away from the demands of your family and the world, in the exotic spa that is your mouldy bathroom, during the magical time that is called *me*. And a Galaxy isn't just a quick sugar hit with a coffee when you didn't have time for lunch. Oh no. It's a half-hour semi-erotic private experience to be savoured whenever your child goes next door to play. Got some time to yourself? Then consume!

But it *is* just time to ourselves, isn't it? Time when we could read a book, sleep, count buttons, pick our noses or stare into space. A basic human right. Not some material prize for martyring ourselves on the altar of parenthood for which we should be eternally grateful. Not time that should have to be negotiated or earned. I don't want to be made to feel thankful for being bought a bath bomb and being allowed an hour of a Saturday morning to use it. I'd be spending half of my allotted 'me time' fishing wet petals out of the plug-hole for starters. No – you can keep your *me time*, or your *you time*. Whatever it is. But I'm definitely up for that Sunday walk and pub lunch next month. Without the kids, of course. Just me and some old friends. Three hours of *quality time*. Yes, that'll do me fine. And what's more, I'll do five consecutive early mornings and a trip to the in-laws to get it.

MILESTONES

If you are lucky enough to be a first-born child, your life will be positively crammed with milestones. Every tiny step on your developmental journey will be catalogued and applauded by your obsessive parents. It's just all so damned significant.

There's birth, obviously a big one, then smiling (because of wind), smiling again (because you actually want to), sleeping through, raking a raisin, weaning, sitting up, first time on the swing, first time in the car seat, first time on a train, first time on a bus, crawling, cruising, walking, talking, talking while walking, managing a big spoon, drinking from a cup with a lid, drinking from a cup without a lid, drinking from a straw in a cup without a lid . . .

Of course, if you are a second born, you have no milestones. You simply grow up, slightly in your parents' peripheral vision, and can expect no fanfare when you dribble for the first time from the right side of your mouth instead of the left. They may just about look up when you take your first steps, it may merit a photo, if they can only remember where the camera is . . .

Milestones are very much the stuff of early childhood, and whether you are first born or subsequent, they become less frequent once you start school. Teenage years involve a few key legal milestones, like being able to drink, drive (not at the same time – that's dangerous), vote, marry. Then? Nothing. No further milestones. Nature tires of hurling us through new developmental thresholds every few months and life becomes a lot more old-doggy and a lot less new-tricksy.

To replace milestones, adults instead have: millstones, kidney stones, I'm stoned, my scones.

MINE

An important first word in a child's vocabulary. Rarely used as in 'what's mine is yours'. And they're not talking about underground excavations, either.

MMR

You've read quite a few snippets of anecdotal evidence about autistic regression following the single jab. Your child currently gets his kicks watching the pants go round and round in your Servis Automatic so you're a little bit worried on that score. Perhaps you could take the middle path between total denial and total paranoia. You could go private. Just in case. Opt for the three single jabs. Just in case. And wouldn't you be impressed! The distraction techniques are so much more sophisticated at a private clinic. No more nurses lamely clicking their fingers and playing peekaboo. Now there is a team of two – a doctor to do the dirty deed and a nurse solely for personal entertainment. She's got a veritable circus of equipment, too: bubble-machines, balloons and blowy whistles. Oh yes indeed – it's a vaccination party! Junior won't even notice as the needle plunges in – he'll be too busy squealing with rapture as the nurse cartwheels past him. Which is just as well because he'll have to go through it all again. Twice. And then do it all over again for the boosters in two years' time.

The boosters? Bugger. No, no one ever mentioned the boosters. At £100 a pop, and with that man Wakefield now discredited, it's *you* who'll be feeling the prick.

MORO REFLEX

In babies: startle reflex which stops new babies falling out of imaginary trees – signifies healthy reactions and primitive instinctive behaviours.

In adults: startle reflex in REM phase of sleep which causes new parents to dive off ends of beds to catch and rock imaginary falling babies whilst real babies slumber safely in cots. Signifies sleep-deprived reactions and totally looped-out stressed behaviours.

N n

NCT CLASSES

NCT antenatal classes are hugely popular. Like primary schools with outstanding Ofsted reports or Shoreditch House, they are oversubscribed and have long waiting lists. If you fail to get on to an NCT class you may panic and assume that all lucky participants will have serene, kharmic births because they have had the truth and the light imparted to them, while you are destined for an emergency Caesarean by a hung-over surgeon after a thirty-six-hour labour.

This is not the case. NCT classes do not teach you anything that you cannot read in a book, and, of course, the kind of people that go to them are the ones that have read every book, website and blog on childbirth already. Consequently, the teaching your grandmother to suck eggs factor is high. In fact, getting granny in with half a dozen free-range would make a pleasing diversion from all the getting-to-know-you exercises and 'what are you hoping to learn?' questions that take up at least three of the six sessions. In addition, you may get to handle a knitted foetus, you may get to practise birthing positions with a bunch of total strangers, and you may get to drink a lot of squash, but really, how can this prepare you for childbirth? Giving birth is like taking your A levels. You can do all the revision, but you can't know what questions will come up. You might get Catholic emancipation, when you were hoping for the Chartists.

At best, you'll make some friends who you can spend hours eating cake and comparing notes with in assorted cafés around town for the next six months, until the first splitter goes back to work and the group dissolves. At worst, you'll squeeze your heavily pregnant body into someone's tiny living room, over-stuffed with other heavily pregnant bodies, for a couple of hours each week and make strained conversation with indi-viduals you have nothing in common with except pregnancy and a recently discovered love of custard creams.

NETWORKING

No longer involving any combination of the words career, licking and arse, or fun, flirting and friends, the new networking is all about survival, not self-promotion; and support, not self-gratification.

Your new network is undeniably female in composition, and the initiation ceremony may possibly involve consuming your own bodyweight in coffee and cake. The only blokes included in it will probably be your child's father (though he is more of a sleeping partner) and Bob, the owner of Bob's local child-friendly café. Your new network consists (almost entirely) of other mums. You will see the (odd) dad lurking awkwardly by the slide in a playground, or having a solitary read of the papers in a café while his child sits strapped in a pushchair squirting juice up his nose and the wall, but they are much less frequently spotted at the major parenting network hubs: baby and toddler groups. Well, you can understand it really. You too would feel mightily embarrassed if you were a lone, off-pitch baritone singing 'She'll Be Coming Round The Mountain' amongst a chorus of fairly tuneful sopranos. While skipping.

So, it's just you and the mums. You don't have to be alike, or even like each other, of course. The only criteria for entry to this network are whether you live locally and your children are the same age. You desperately try to force friendships on your asocial eight-month-old because it enables you to meet up with another two mothers of eight-month-olds in a café. Which means you can happily while away two hours chatting about how strange babies are and drinking coffee while your offspring hit each other over the heads with spoons. At least it gets you out of the house. Although you may still have to spend many winter days freezing your bits off in a playground, you feel oh so much better if someone else is with you, freezing theirs off in solidarity. And not only does it alleviate the tedium of caring for kids, it is actually quite nice; refreshing even. It's just that it seems a teensy bit weird. Sometimes you get the feeling that the real you is in a parallel universe somewhere drinking lager with a bloke called Dan.

In the 'old' days, of course, the parenting network would have been based on *faaammily*. Yours would too if you hadn't slashed your familial ties and buggered off as far as your Young Person's Railcard would carry you at the first adult opportunity. It is only when you face that first day alone in the house with the twin horrors of a new baby and Jeremy Kyle for company that you wish your mum and dad lived next door, like Ken and Deirdre Barlow. You feel this even more acutely when it comes to considering your babysitting and childcare options further down the line.

Luckily, your early caffeine and nursery-rhyme based forays into parental networking will have paid off. You are entering the era of the reciprocal arrangement. Caroline down the road will happily look after your delightful child for one day a week (hooray!). Unfortunately, this means you will have to look after Caroline 'the princess' junior for one day a week in return. Well, come on. You can't have your cake and eat it. You've got to share, you know.

NEW NORMAL

You've had a baby and secretly you're just waiting for life to 'get back to normal'. Well, that normal is the old normal and it's gone for good. The new normal is a noxious mix of the incredibly mundane and the incredibly stressful. A lot of picking things up off the floor, aimless buggy-pushing and

repeating yourself, punctuated by late-night dashes to A&E
and lashings of vomit. It's just not normal at all.

NIGHT DRIVING

You're going to Cornwall or Scotland or somewhere over two
hours away and you think, How are we going to drive this,
with children? The answer, for many parents, is to set off at
night. In fact, the post-9 p.m. motorways of Britain are used
only by weary salesmen, the emergency services and families
attempting slightly ambitious journeys.

It's just so much easier to go at night, isn't it? Easier, but not
easy. It's a relative term. In this case, going at night is the difference between a pretty shit option and a really shit option. Your
child will hopefully sleep, so that sidesteps all the usual car
journey brouhaha that characterises most daytime excursions
(see Car Journeys). What it does not sidestep is the fact that you
are now tackling a long-distance drive at the time of day when
you would usually be having a second glass of Rioja and thinking
about a bath. Plus, it's darker than Satan's armpit out there.

You'll arrive at your destination at midnight, wide-eyed and
buzzed and dying for a piss, having nearly hit two sheep and
driven through a blizzard of moths. Don't relax yet, though,
because you have to unpack the car in the dark and settle your
kids into bed, and they can't decide whether to run around
excitedly or cling to you in despair. Then, when you finally
get to bed, headlights burnt onto your retina, you'll be
breaking sharply in your sleep and dream-steering your way

round hairpin bends. Which, even if you're Lewis Hamilton, is not the definition of a good night's sleep. See, it's easier to go at night. But not easy.

NIT PICKING

Literally, picking nits.

Starting school is a big time in a child's life. It's also a big time in a head louse's life as it signals the beginning of 'the season' for the head lice community, during which period they can wander merrily from reception head to reception head, pumping out eggs like ammo from an AK47 and boosting the head lice population by about 12,000 per cent.

The first time you spot a head louse on your child's head is a rite of passage. You never forget it. You might feel a bit shaky, but you keep cool because you've read the school photocopy illustrated with the comedy cartoon nit, impaled on a comb. Like George Bush when he invaded Iraq, you are confident it will all be over by Christmas.

But head lice, or 'naughty nits' as we call them in my house, in an attempt to put a 'fun' spin on an infestation, are tenacious. Leave just a single egg behind on one of your combing missions and within the week your child's head is hopping again. You can drench his scalp in toxic mousse and foul-smelling remedies but, like those freaky rats that mutate and survive a nuclear bomb, one bionic head louse will always crawl free of the debris, dust itself off and start egging it up all over again.

The only consolation is that once you get over your initial revulsion, picking head lice out of your child's hair can be fun. Almost relaxing. And what a fascinating illustration of our genetic proximity to chimps. Human mum and ape mum, united in a shared drive to rid our offspring of lice. Only we don't eat them.

NOT SWEARING . . .

It's bloody frustrating.

Most parents agree that swearing in front of young children is not big or clever. And yet it still happens, because we are all flawed individuals and because having young children throws up so many opportunities for a ripe and colourful expletive.

When it comes to swearing, there are a number of variations. There's swearing in the vicinity of your children, so that poor language hovers over them like a kind of miasma, but without directly implicating them, and there is swearing at them, which never makes you feel good about yourself. No three-year-old deserves to be called a twat. Well, not out loud, anyway.

Some of us can control our tongues while indoors or in public, but get behind the wheel of a car and Jesus fucking Christ – a torrent of filth will gush from our lips, because every other bastard on the road is out to sodding cut us up. Which prompts other adults in the car to shriek at us to mind our bloody language. In front of the bloody kids. It's a swearing bonanza!

A useful tip is to sit down with your partner and draw up a list of Just About OK and Definitely Not Cool swear words, to act as a ready reminder. So, for instance, in my household we've agreed you can bugger it, sod it and arse it, but you cannot fuck it. You're allowed a bloody hell, but not a cunting bum, and two bollocks are roughly equal to a bastard.

If you are very lucky, your child will rise above all this vulgarity and refrain from swearing themselves. Mostly, mine are blasé about my low-rent vocabulary and pretty polite. Although there was that time my son told me he didn't always wash his hands after a wee at nursery because he 'couldn't be fucked'. I made it clear to him that this was a bad word, that should never be used by children or adults. He got quite into that idea and suggested we put up a big sign in the hall saying NO FUCKING.

I must get that sorted out . . .

NO WIN

You really want to share parenthood with your partner, but you're just so much better at it than him.

O o

ORGANIC

It may be organic, but if they're not going to eat it anyway, that's just some very expensive carrots you've tossed in the bin.

ORGANISATION

It's quite simple. If you know *exactly* what you're doing. Like a Rubik's Cube. I work part time, so elder child goes to after-school club on Tuesdays and Wednesdays. On Tuesdays, Kate from up the road takes him and her own child home and gives them tea, unless she's got to collect her youngest from swimming (only once a fortnight), in which case I ask retired neighbour to collect and mind him for half an hour (she *doesn't* give him tea), by which time I should be back from work, having picked up younger one from nursery. On Wednesdays, local childminder does pick-up and tea and will occasionally collect younger child from nursery, too, so I can work later, but cannot confirm this until Monday of each week, due to her own pressing social life. Partner does nursery drop-off on Tuesday, I do school, but on Wednesdays I do both, because he has to get an early train. On Fridays elder child has Kung Fu, which starts at 6 p.m. This is too late for younger one, so I meet partner at station to hand her over and they go home in taxi, while I drop elder one at class then nip to Tesco Metro for weekend food. It's all fine. Unless childminder gets ill. Or Kate from up the road. Or children. Or husband. Or me. Then it's not fine. Or simple. At all.

OTHER PEOPLE'S CHILDREN

It's hard enough to like your own sometimes, but other people's?

The problem is you don't have to like kids to have kids. Nature makes sure you like your own – well, at least some of the time – but it doesn't fit you with a universal good-will-to-all-children gene. You can like them in the broadest sense, as in, you approve of their presence in the world, but essentially, you can remain a non-liker of kids even after you have some.

Now this is a pain, because having kids will bring you into contact with legions of other kids. Not since you were a kid yourself have you had to hang out with so many kids. And other people's kids can be so weird. Some stare at you when you talk to them like you are speaking Swahili. Some ignore you. Some let you wipe their mouths or noses without saying thanks.

Perhaps they're embarrassed? I doubt it. Most don't know your name and have zero interest in finding out.

Other people's children are often absolutely hopeless when removed from familiar surroundings, too. A four-year-old's frame of reference is very small, so hanging out round yours is the equivalent of crash landing in Burkina Faso. It's all so different, but different isn't good. Why have you chopped up my banana? I only eat them whole – that's how Mummy does it. I will now eye you with suspicion and unease. Banana-chopper-upper-freak.

You have to be on your best behaviour around other people's kids, too, and may feel awkwardly self-conscious. Dealing with any sub-optimal behaviour is difficult. After all, they could totally dob on you to their mum if you snap at them. Dealing with accidents, ditto. If they wet themselves whilst in your care, you have to be chirpy and sympathetic, whereas if it was your own child you could cuss them under your breath and yank at their pants with poorly disguised disgust. You have to listen to their stories, their cheek, their lies ('I don't have to be strapped in when I'm in Daddy's car') with a thin smile, not a dismissive put-down. It all stretches the limits of your child-friendliness to the ruddy max.

Grappling with other people's kids (not literally, but oh, how much fun that could be . . .) is particularly tricksy when you really love their parents. They're your best mates, but you are having to work extra hard to find the same charm in their kids. With a bit of effort you may come to find their children bearable, but it's just so much easier to find them annoying. Them and all their other little friends.

OVER-DEVELOPED LEFT ARM

Think of an arm. Then double it. That's your arm, that is. Or will be once you have a child. For all the slings, hip-seats and buggies you might have purchased, the most reliable form of transport for your child is your left arm. Useful for rapid scooping and all short journeys. It's hard at first, of course. You struggle to get to the end of the road without your 7lb newborn slipping dangerously down to your knee. Your left arm's only used to holding your mobile and a fag so it's not really up to the job yet. But it soon will be. A constant daily workout with an increasingly heavy baby will provide you with a significantly enlarged and finely defined bicep. Shame it's just the one though. Looking like a Gladiator from the left and Amy Winehouse from the right, you might not look so great in that halterneck this year. But you will be able to carry a sack of spuds whilst hoovering, so that just about makes up for it.

OVER-QUALIFIED

You may find that when you try to return to work after children the only jobs available are ever so slightly beneath your capabilities. Strictly speaking, you don't need a Ph.D. to work mornings doing admin in the office of a packaging distributor on an industrial estate, but of course it may help get the attention of the interview panel in the first place, so that's useful.

P p

PARENTING BOOKS

Gosh, there are a lot of them about.

There's the serious sociological investigation. You know the ones. Man alive, it's grim out there for parents. You'll be down Tesco doing the family shop with a butchered fanny three days after giving birth, in pain, alone and desperate. And it gets worse. AWOL dads, depressed mums, doolally kids out of their minds on Sunny D and Ventolin inhalers. These books are very valid, great for masochists and intellectuals, or masochistic intellectuals, but not exactly a light holiday read.

Then there's the humorous guide. You'll probably follow some hapless woman through her pregnancy, with lots of comedy detail about her piles and her skin tags, a blow-by-blow account of the birth followed by some handy tips about how to handle the first few weeks. Fit some blackout blinds and ask a friend to do the shopping for you. That sort of thing. The jackets of these books promise straight talk, practical tips and hilarious tales. It's just like your best mate telling you how it is, isn't it? Only much more irritating and much less helpful.

Then there's the advice-heavy parenting manual. There are thousands of them in the bookshops, each one utterly counter-productive and a source of much anxiety. They tell you that there is a way to do it, which probably means you're doing it wrong. And which 'way' do you choose? Do you go continuum concept or strict routine, or somewhere in between? Most women, having spent £45 on assorted confidence-shattering tomes, go for the muddle-through approach. And you can't write a manual for that.

Finally, there's the self-indulgent first-person memoir of the early years of parenthood. It's packed with side-splitting accounts of how the writer's mother-in-law mistakenly used a breast pad as a coaster, the toddler was rushed to Casualty with a plastic gorilla jammed in its ear and the baby puked all over the posh friend's Armani suit. Plus, there's always lots of rushing, running and juggling, as if parenthood is perpetually like the closing sequence of an episode of The Benny Hill Show. And the covers . . . All wacky writing and cute little cartoons. Each chapter heading looks like it was penned by someone with really fat fingers grappling with a Berol marker. On a train. Do we lose our powers of aesthetic discernment just because we have kids? Dear God, show us some respect.

PARENTING PROGRAMMES

You're not going to learn anything new by watching them. People have been timing out their kids since Jesus was in nappies. They're just designed to bring out the shameless voyeur and smug git in all of us. I mean, for crying out loud, thirty-two yogurts in one day!

PARKS

Somewhere to smoke and drink cider in when you're a teenager. Avoided thereafter until you have kids, whereupon they become as familiar as your own trousers.

PART-TIME JOBS

Children are expensive. Once you embrace motherhood, unless you are a full-time career high-flier with 'staff' like Nicola Horlick, or are married to an insolvency lawyer, say, and can afford to stay at home revelling in well-heeled domestic bliss, you are likely to be doing, or at least thinking about doing, some sort of part-time work.

78 per cent of part-time workers in Britain are women* and two-thirds of women who are working with dependent children have part-time careers.** Whoops, I mean jobs. Silly me,

* Equal Opportunities Commission 2005
**Office for National Statistics 2005

after all, it's quite easy to tell them apart. Careers are those things women have in their twenties. They provide boring practical essentials like rights and pensions, promotion prospects and salary progression, and sometimes more exciting perks like a bit of intellectual stimulation, a smattering of foreign travel and the occasional chance to wear sharp suits and killer heels. (Perk three becomes quite important in retrospect when you realise you have worn jeans and Converse every day for three years.) These careers usually require you to work full time.

Proper part-time jobs, however, are a teensy bit different. A third to a half of women working part time are working in jobs below their qualifications and potential. They are more likely to be working in distribution, hotel and catering, banking (and no, we're not talking hedge fund managers here, funnily enough, think more stamping deposit books in your local HSBC), cleaning, charitable services and in schools and higher education. They receive 40 per cent less training than their full-time counterparts and earn 40 per cent less per hour than men working full time.*

Not fair? Well, we shouldn't be so demanding, should we? If we will insist on working locally, having hours to fit round the school day and flexibility during the school holidays, we can shove our MBAs up our orange overalls and bloody well get on with slicing cheddar at Sainsbury's.

And we do, because often we want, and need, to work. That's why the post of Teaching Assistant has for many mothers become that holy grail: the perfect, interesting-way-to-pay-some-bills-whilst-being-there-for-the-children part-time job. Competition is ferocious. *The Apprentice* looks like a walk in the park compared to this. 'A hundred highly qualified mothers have been whittled down to just sixteen. The candidates will take part in the toughest recruitment process in low-paid part-time employment. Sixteen candidates, two Heads of Year, one Head Teacher and one self-important Chair of Governors.' 'This is the job interview from hell,' quips Head, Alice Sugar. 'Only one can survive to win the coveted £11,900-a-year position.'

And it won't be you. You may have a maths degree (quite useful from a numeracy angle, one might have thought), but the seven hours a week you have spent 'helping out' at school for the past three years does not count as paid work with children. You need to be hugely overqualified AND have several years' paid experience for this job, you muntering fool. Back you go to employment oblivion. So what to do? Bugger it, if all else fails, you'll just have to do what all the other desperado mums out there do. Write a hilarious parenting book or set up your own exclusive internet business selling organic scatter cushions and children's hemp underwear.

As long as you can do it part time, of course.

PATIENCE

Patience is a virtue, apparently, and one thing is certain – having children is when you find out.

The problem is, although vital to parenting, being patient is not rated much in any other arena of life. Fat cats didn't get fat sitting about patiently. They got it by shouting 'NOW!' a lot and throwing their phones around. Women didn't get the vote by patiently waiting for men to be so good as to offer it them. They went on hunger strike and flung themselves in front of galloping racehorses. They had been patient long enough, thank you very much, and it was time for action.

Even people who employ patience at work may like to clock off at the end of the day and let their tetchy, snappy side take over. But of course kids don't adhere to working hours. They expect overtime and weekends, too. It really is enough to try your patience.

All the manuals will tell you it's vital to model patient behaviour for your children. The more patient you can be, the more effective you will be as a parent. Tricky this. It was easy for those Tibetan monks. They only had the Chinese army to deal with . . . You've got to ask your child, quietly and calmly, to get dressed for the fifth time. Just as you did yesterday morning, and the one before that, and the one before that. Plus, of course, you are tired/stressed/late/trying to make a packed lunch, and these additional factors will strip away your last scraps of patience like a bag of Haribo on a two-year-old's tooth enamel.

Sensible parenting books will tell you to take a deep breath, count to ten, leave the room perhaps. But this is not a sensible parenting book so, when you're about to lose it, we would recommend the following:

1. stuffing dry Jacob's crackers into your mouth – stuff, stuff, stuff
2. inserting a pineapple down your trousers (the pain may distract you)
3. watching footage of Meg Ryan on *Parkinson* (again, the pain may distract you)
4. crying
5. calling your partner so he can 'share' the situation
6. reading Gerard Manley Hopkins' poem 'Patience, Hard Thing!' The title is apt, but the rest is devilish tricky stuff about God and wounds and rebellious wills, which might at least take your mind off the fact that your child still hasn't brushed her teeth . . .

PELVIC FLOOR . . . A LAMENT

> Loo loo, nip to the loo
> Loo loo, nip to the loo
> Loo loo, nip to the loo
> Nip to the loo, my darling

Oops. Too late.

PHASES

He's refusing to go to bed, he's going to bed but waking in the night, he's stopped waking in the night but he's waking up early, he's gone off nursery, he's clingy, he's grumpy, he's wetting himself, he's stopped wetting himself, he's snotty, he's spotty, he's straight, he's gay, he's straight again. Life with kids is just a series of phases.

The big mistake is to think that an invisible threshold exists at some point in the future that you cross and suddenly, the clouds part, the sun comes out and you are *there*. No more phases. You've done it. You've arrived. You get your photo in the local paper, the Queen sends you a telegram and, wow, what a feeling, because you've put the years of work in, taken the knocks, suffered the setbacks but at last, you're done. Everyone gets themselves dressed in the morning, everyone can brush their teeth without help, no more buggies, no more nappies, no more tannies.

Explain this idea to parents of much older children and they will laugh wryly and shake their heads. The parenting nirvana of which you dream does not exist. Life with children carries on being hard, but in different ways. These same parents may even look back fondly to the days when they had children under six years old. Yes, it was relentless and maddening, but at least they liked a cuddle back then.

Coming to this realisation is truly depressing. It's like discovering that Father Christmas doesn't exist. Or that babies don't come out of your belly button. Or that Jimmy Krankie was actually a woman. A really small one.

PLAYDATE: THE DIARY OF A
BY A MUM AGED 37¾

1 p.m. Shop for inoffensive foodstuffs and suitably exciting pudding items. Not forgetting litre bottle of ketchup!

1.30 p.m. Clean house from top to bottom. Other child's parent coming to collect. Don't want her to know we live like pigs. Need to clean more than just hall and living room in case other child tells her there are pants all over bedroom floor and bathroom smells like poo.

3 p.m. Collect children from school. Have what feels like heart attack on seven-minute walk home as other child swings round lamp-post into path of oncoming vehicle. (Maybe also something to do with carrying two coats, two jumpers, two book-bags, two lunchboxes and a 3-foot cardboard lighthouse?) Begin to understand why other people drive half a mile to school. Resolve to bugger environment and take driving lessons.

3.07 p.m. Enter house.

3.08 p.m. Children ask if can watch television. Say no.

3.09 p.m. Children enter garden to play football and collect snails.

3.11 p.m. Children return to house.

3.12 p.m. Children rush up to son's bedroom. Empty out drawers. Bang drum and strum guitar.

3.15 p.m. Children have argument.

3.16 p.m. Children come downstairs and say they are bored.
Clench teeth, check watch.

3.17 p.m. Get children juice and biscuits. Children play spitting over Laura Ashley rug. Not good, but at least not arguing.

3.34 p.m. Children ask if can watch television. Say no.

3.35 p.m. Suggest children play with balloons. Blow up two. Son disappoints by having tantrum over randomly allotted balloon colour. Other child irritates by correctly suggesting son is bad at sharing because he is only child.

3.40 p.m. Balloon game successfully under way. Escape to computer . . . Maybe should re-register with Facebook . . .

3.44 p.m. Balloon pops. Son cries. Demands other child's balloon. Says it's other child's fault. Blood pressure rises and mental stability feels fragile. Decide to go to park, even though wet.

3.46 p.m. Ignore argument over allocation of bike/scooter.

3.55 p.m. Arrive at park. Buy coffee and sit on wet bench. Make few phone calls in attempt to ignore children while they play/fight/argue.

4.35 p.m. Rain too heavy. Bottom and children wet. Decide to return home. Engage fully in argument over allocation of bike/scooter. Decide to send son to naughty stair on return to think about behaviour. Other child infuriates by correctly suggesting son is bad at turn-taking because he is only child.

4.45 p.m. Retreat to kitchen to prepare fishfingers. Ask other child if he likes potatoes, broccoli and carrots. Assures he does.

4.46 p.m. Children ask if can watch television. Say no and ask them to lay table.

5.00 p.m. Serve up meal. Ignore argument about plate allocation. Smile and say, 'Enjoy!' Other child says actually he doesn't like potatoes, broccoli and carrots, after all. Realise would be very wrong to shout at someone else's child. Leave room and consider jumping out of bedroom window.

5.15 p.m. Return to take plates. Finish off cold fishfingers and tip slick of ketchup and vegetables into bin. Serve strawberries and ice-cream. Children happy. Children play spitting over table.

5.30 p.m. Children say they are bored. Ask if can watch television. Say yes.

6.00 p.m. Pace floor waiting for other parent to arrive.

6.11 p.m. Other parent arrives. Tell her children have only just started watching television. Smile and say children have been 'fine', though admit son might have been a little 'territorial'. Parent and child finally leave fifteen minutes later after child extracted from behind sofa, shoes wedged onto feet and bags thrust into hands.

6.24 p.m. Retreat to kitchen. Reflect on inability to control and/or entertain two four-year-old boys. Despair of further confirmation of bad parenting skills.

6.25 p.m. Consider opening wine.

6.26 p.m. Open wine.

PLAYING

It should be fun. Play is fun, right? But God, it's so *hard*, it's almost unbearable. The worst thing a kid can say to you is not 'you don't love me' but 'can you play with me?' I would rather be made to listen to every edition of *You & Yours* ever broadcast, on a loop, than play with my kids. There, I've said it.

Before you have children you think playing with them is what it's all about. Once you have them, you realise it is, in fact, a special brand of torture devised by young people to inflict upon adults. Well, they want to play such stupid stuff. I'm too old to go running up the corridor in search of baddies, OK? I'm thirty-seven, for crap's sake. I can't fly like Superman, even if I do make a cape out of a beach towel. And, oh Christ, do we have to take the register again, 'Teacher'? How many times, already?

There is also always the risk that you will be 'doing it wrong', which really flips your kid out, but is hard to avoid since the rules are unclear/only exist in your child's head/are so bloody ridiculous you can't follow them. So the whole act of playing can descend into outraged and heated exchanges between you and your child, which is just a giant pain in the arse for both of you.

Admittedly, some of the problems with playing are our own. We feel self-conscious and silly. We're not used to acting and big gestures and we never have the stamina or enthusiasm to play for as long as they want. Early-years experts say that half an hour of immersing yourself in your child's game, doing absolutely whatever they want, is more valuable than hours of saying 'that's nice, dear' while you try to sort out the laundry. But half an hour! You *are* joking. Five minutes feels like an eternity. You want thirty? It's just so so so boring. I don't mind a jigsaw puzzle and I can just about manage some throw and catch, but anything else makes me feel so fidgety and oppressed that I want to scream or cry or both.

Basically, kids need to play with each other, not us. When are they going to realise?

POO

Maybe you were once a bit squeamish about matters of the bottom. Not one for a backwards glance down the toilet bowl, or scatological humour (though you must admit, that joke involving the bum hole and the lettuce is quite funny*).

Having children, however, is like undergoing rapid and prolonged exposure therapy for your faecal phobia, but without the professional support of a trained psychotherapist. Well, it *is* pretty shitty from the word go and, unfortunately, impossible to change a nappy with your eyes shut whilst holding your nose and retching. So you just have to be sensible and get on with it. At first you do it using disposable gloves, half a pack of wipes, an inflatable changing

---

* A man walks into a doctor's with some lettuce hanging out of his bottom. The doctor examines him and carefully considers his diagnosis. 'I'm very sorry to have to tell you this, sir,' he says gravely, 'but it's just the tip of the iceberg.'

mat and a well-ventilated room. But before you know it, you've become blasé about poo. You're in a café, having a good hooter full (*see also* Sniffing babies' arses) then changing the nappy on a chair using a serviette as a wipe and your Top Shop cardie as a changing mat. Your house smells like poo, too, by the way, but if you stay in it for long enough you won't notice. (*See also* Depression and Loneliness.)

Don't think it's over once they are toilet trained, either. Nappy changing merely gives way to stinky bum-wiping and pooey-pant washing. You'll be in the shit for some time to come. Get used to it.

Now, did I tell you the one about the cannibal who dumped his girlfriend?

POP

Have kids, will not pop.

The idea of popping anywhere when you have children is laughable. They can raise the simplest errand to the corner shop into a veritable pantomime of fannying: whingeing about going, hunting for coats, someone needing a wee, cajoling them into their shoes, walking really slowly, someone tripping up and crying, having to carry the little one, a litany of grumbles from the big one . . . All this for two pints of semi-skimmed.

This is how you fail to pick up the essential items that previously you would have just popped out for. The stamps and picture hooks and birthday cards and parking permits. There were enough hours in the day, the distance to the shops was negligible, but with kids it all suddenly became impossibly difficult to just pop and do it.

POST-NATAL

Congratulations! You did it! You made it through the birth. You endured the pain and the blood and the bizarre indignity of flashing your extremities to all-comers magnificently. Phewee! Bet you're glad that's all over. Now you can relax and get all snuggly with your newborn. You can, can't you? No? Woah! Hang on there! Don't get all soft-focus on us yet. There's a bit more pain, a lot more blood and another flurry of flashing to undergo first.

Oh bugger. You spent so long focusing on the Natal that you forgot to think about the Post.

Nobody told you that you will feel (and look, judging by my photos) as though you've ridden a particularly boisterous colt naked and bare-back across the Pennines and then had a car crash on the way home. At a time when you thought you might be doing a lot of cuddling and cooing, you are actually doing a significant amount of ouching and wincing. For the first time in your life, you come to a full appreciation of the meaning of the adverb *gingerly*. Having never previously experienced stitches in your nether regions, you're ignorant of the fact that this will cause you to hobble bow-legged like John Wayne and mean you have to wee in the bath for the next four weeks to stop yourself from shooting through the roof whenever the uric acid touches those sore bits.

You were also completely unaware of the fact that having a baby through your vagina might somehow adversely affect your bottom. That indeed, passing a 5-ounce stool post-birth will be just as toe-curlingly painful as giving birth to an 8-pound baby. What the hell is a perineum anyway? Unfortunately, there are no epidurals or pethidine shots available to you when defecating in that four-week recovery period so you just have to pop a paracetamol and employ the deep breathing techniques that you forgot to use during the birth. You briefly consider hypno-pooing, but eventually opt for blaspheming heavily and crying instead.

To add insult to injury, you may well be obliged to undergo these indignities on a post-natal ward rather than in the sanct-ity of your own home. Which means a quarter of a mile to the nearest toilet, crap food and twelve other women tutting at your maternal ineptitude. And the only person who you feel might be able to support you through the terror of these first few nights has been packed off home promptly at 8 p.m. to go and drink Champagne and congratulate himself on his impressive virility. New motherhood, as Greg Wallace might say, *doesn't get tougher than this*.

Luckily, even if you are recovering from a Caesarean or some other bit of junior doctor's needlework, they will soon whip the sheets out from under your sore bott and send you home to free up a bed. Great. At last you can get on with letting your body recover and find your feet in the mother-ing business in private. Well, you could if it wasn't for the legions of well-meaning relatives and friends who turn up with flowers that need putting in vases, expecting cups of tea, sometimes lunch, and thoughtfully enquiring after the soreness of your undercarriage. Getting an angsty newborn to latch on to your inexperienced boob is tricky enough without having to do it in front of your Uncle Brian.

Reassuringly, though, a kindly midwife you've never seen before will visit you in those first few days to check that you and your baby are doing OK. There you'll be, sitting together, having a nice chat and a cuppa – perhaps even a custard cream – when like a bolt out of the blue she'll ask to have a quick shufti at your nethers. In your front room! At 10 a.m.! Jesus! Has the woman no morals?! You thought she was your friend! You didn't see that one coming. It's also a shame that the postman happens to be strolling past the window with an armful of cards at the time. Ah, what the hell! It feels like the rest of the south coast has seen your Mrs Craddock. The more the merrier . . .

PRE-EMPTING

Your job as a mother is not simply to love and nurture your children, it is to become a psychic, who can see twelve hours into the future and precisely predict the 'stuff' that will be needed to cover whatever bonkers eventuality gets thrown your way. But here's the bad news: you will always fail at this. Thus life becomes frighteningly like an episode of *The Weakest Link*.

You remembered to buy snacks for the journey. BANK. And cartons of juice. BANK. And to locate their favourite car colouring-pad, even though it was under the driver's seat. BANK. You anticipated that your son might puke halfway there, so packed clean clothes. BANK. And he did puke and you were totally prepared for it – yes! BANK. On arriving at your friends' house, your son suddenly remembered that he wanted to bring his sonic screwdriver to show the other kids, but it's OK because you remembered and it's in the bag that also contains clean pants for your youngest in case he craps himself, and clean socks in case he pees on his feet, which he might, so BANK. You brought some of their favourite biscuits in case they wouldn't eat lunch. BANK. And the little one's wellies as he sometimes refuses to go outside in his shoes. BANK. You even packed the scooter. BANK. Which is good because we're making an unscheduled trip to the park. BANK. But, oh no, oh no, oh no, the clouds are clearing, the sun's coming out and ARRGGGHHHHH! You forgot the sun-cream! You only went and forgot the sun-cream! What? It was cloudy this morning? That's no excuse. You should have guessed it would clear up. You should have checked the weather forecast. You should have known.

You are the weakest link, goodbye!

QUAVERS

Do the job of crisps without actually being crisps. A convenient mid-point between full-on Salt & Vinegar and organic
baked puffs. Made of crisped and flavoured air, and with only
87 calories a bag, you can tell yourself they're almost healthy,
too. (*See also* Wotsits.)

QUEUING

To be feared when you have children. Like celebrities or the
Queen, kids don't 'do' queuing.

QUIET

Like a doodlebug bomb, it's when they go quiet that
you're in trouble. Five minutes' quiet means peaceful

colouring in their room, six means you'll need to redecorate the landing.

QUIRKS

Children are wonderfully quirky. Maybe it's their way of asserting control over their tiny little lives, but they certainly seem to be mad for minutiae. The devil is definitely in the detail when it comes to their behaviour. No issue is too small for a big old barney. They develop so many strange obsessions and demands that you feel like you're dealing with a premenstrual J-Lo's backstage rider on a daily basis.

For dinner she wants the sweetcorn next to the peas (but not touching the sausages), the pink plate (not the yellow), and to sit next to Daddy (but not opposite the door, doh!). When going out he may well insist on wearing sandals when it's pissing down, with or without socks and a Power Ranger mask, depending on whether Johnny up the road has passed your window wearing a policeman's helmet. He would also like to carry his 2-foot pirate's cutlass. On all journeys. For maybe forty-five seconds until he suggests quite strongly that you carry it. You could acquiesce to most of these demands, of course. They're only petty inconveniences, after all, and perhaps you worry that he'll become immune to the word no if you say it 122 times a day. You'd rather save it for the really important things, like when he's throwing bottles at next door's cat or playing Bob the Builder with the very sharp side of the bread knife at your dining table.

If you're bored and feeling a little contrary yourself, however, you might prefer to argue the toss. If so, get creative. There are many interesting ways of saying no. Think of it as a vocabulary-expanding, problem-solving challenge. When you don't want her to wear her high-heeled sparkly dressing-up sandals for walking the dog, tell her that although it may offend her highly developed aesthetic sensibilities, the wellies would be far more appropriate.

And if that doesn't work, tell her 'because I said so'. Guaranteed to precipitate a tanny of such biblical proportions that you'll forget that the dog needed walking anyway. And it will satisfy that arsey argumentative streak in the both of you.

Result.

R r

RABBIT

Chas and Dave contributed much to British culture via their chirpy Cok-er-ney sing-a-long anthems: an appreciation of Margate, in 'Margate'; of Snooker, in 'Snooker Loopy'; and of marriage in 'In Sickness And In Health'. But their Top Ten hit 'Rabbit' though no doubt aimed at an over-communicative spouse, could just as easily be about life with a four-year-old, including as it does, lines like these:

'Rabbit, rabbit, rabbit, rabbit, rabbit, rabbit, rabbit, yap, yap, rabbit, rabbit/
You've got more rabbit than Sainsbury's, why don't you give it a rest?/

With your incessant talking, you're becoming a pest/
Rabbit, rabbit, rabbit, etc.'

Amen to that Chas. Amen to that Dave.

RAISINS

Nutritional snack championed by the fruit-loving middle
classes. Until their child's first dental appointment.

RASHES

They are usually pre- or post-viral rashes. Or heat rash. But all
you can think is, MENINGITIS, MENINGITIS, MENINGITIS!

REAL-LIFE BIRTH STORIES

Blimey, we all know that childbirth is like driving a tank down
a cycle lane. But when we are pregnant, knowing isn't enough.
We hunger for more. More screaming, more gore, more babies.
We want real-life birth stories. We feel a bit grubby and voyeuristic
about wanting them. But we just can't get enough. It all feels
a bit top shelf. Roll up, pregnant women, get your porn fix here:

1. Twenty-four-hour rolling birth programmes on
   Discovery Health. In which desperate women holler
   for mercy with legs splayed and bums in the air,
   followed by tear-jerking scenes with cute babies

popping out. Highly recommended for sado-masochists, masochists and sentimentalists alike.

2. Internet pregnancy chat forums. In which women post blow-by-blow real-time accounts of their labours. Recommended for anal retentives – you too can time their contractions! – and thrill-seekers – you just can't beat that online while on-all-fours tension. Ultimately disappointing when mum-to-be goes offline to push. No one has yet managed to post whilst crowning, so you might just feel a bit cheated.

3. Members of your NCT group. Once they've popped, they just can't stop. You'll be fully acquainted with Lucy's ravaged undercarriage before you've even learnt her surname. Perfect for those who want to hear what birth is really like in their local hospital. Not so good for those who favour the ostrich/head/sand approach.

REASONING

You can spend fifteen minutes setting out a reasoned explanation for why she should be doing this not that, and she will simply turn to you and say, 'But I just want to.'

REGRET

People will tell you that it's not possible to regret having children. It is. It's just one of those sentences you rarely catch anyone saying. Average dinner-party conversation does not go: 'We're thinking of going to France this summer. Oh, and did I mention that I regret having children?'

On the plus side, though, you will probably only experience regret fleetingly, like a stitch or déjà vu, and when you do, it is probably not regretting your *actual* child, but regretting *having* a child (it's subtle, but valid).

As a new parent, you may feel that society has sold you a bit of a porky, banging on as it does about how jolly rewarding having kids is, when you're finding it an overwhelming slog with only tiny snatches of joy thrown in. Months into the parenting game and you may find you are tired, broke and cut off from the real world. Society will still be nodding and winking conspiratorially at you, elbowing you in the ribs going, 'ace, isn't it? best thing ever', while at the same time favouring the childless, with its un-buggy-friendly shops, un-child-friendly restaurants and un-school-friendly working hours. So even though you may be surrounded by other parents pushing other buggies, you can feel very alone in a society that still values personal freedom over familial responsibility.

The really wacky thing about children and regret is that you can also begin to regret your future, as well as your past. You are now welded to a future full of worry and never-ending responsibility. You can dread a lifetime of new issues to be bothered about, from have they eaten enough veg today, to do they hate me and are they doing crack tomorrow. You can very easily regret the amount of money they are going to ask you for as they march through early adulthood and you can also regret the fact that if they grow up to have a complicated or ambivalent relationship with you, it's going to be at least 50 per cent your fault.

Much of the regret that parents feel is bound up in mourning their pre-baby life. Not just the shallow freedoms of doing what you wanted when you wanted. Actually, yes, definitely those shallow freedoms, but also your old face (your new one is more liney), old figure, old wardrobe, old amount of time you would spend in the shower, old relationship and old brain, with its lack of clutter cluttering it.

You will almost certainly regret the things you didn't do when you had the chance. Now, you have no chance. You are too busy laying down your life for another, like Sir Walter Raleigh for Queen Elizabeth. Oh no, hang on, that was his cloak . . .

But let's look at it the other way. If you didn't have children, you'd regret it for the rest of your life, wouldn't you? Yes, but you would do it on a full night's sleep: and that three-week break in Thailand you've got booked might ease your pain. In addition, the mental clarity you have when you don't spend several hours each day wondering what to make your child for tea and where his library book has gone would help you get some perspective. It's true, people with children say they've never known a love like it, but they've never been so tired, skint and bored, either. And just look at those crow's feet . . .

At this point, step forward existential Danish philosopher Kierkegaard, who could have been talking about having kids when he said: 'There are two possible situations – one can either do this or do that. My honest opinion and my friendly advice is this: do it or do not do it – you will regret both.' And then he wandered off to eat a Danish pastry. Which he instantly regretted, because he was on Atkins. But if he hadn't eaten it, he would have regretted that, too, because for two minutes of his otherwise boring afternoon, it filled his mouth with sweetness.

REPEATING YOURSELF

I've asked you once already to get dressed, can you get dressed please. I've asked you three times already. This is the fifth time I've asked you . . .

RE-TRAIN

'I could always re-train . . .'

It's a bit of a mantra for mums who have stepped away from the workplace. They admit they don't know what dropping out of employment or going part time once they have kids means for their career future, but then again, they say, 'I could always re-train . . .'

This sentence is followed by the mum looking off into the middle distance, thoughtfully twiddling a lock of hair, muttering 'midwifery or garden design?' under her breath.

Or it's followed by a wry laugh. Because you know and she knows she hasn't got a clue what to re-train in, or how, or with what money, but it feels good to be saying it all the same.

You also know and she also knows that there are bugger all good part-time jobs out there, even fewer that would use the experience she already has, but re-training, by its very vagueness, offers a little ray of hope, the suggestion of a second chance, a fresh start, a resurrection.

Re-training isn't fast or cheap or easy, which means it is the complete opposite of an ideal option for any parent, who needs things to be fast, cheap and easy.

You could spend four years on some part-time, distance-learning course; four years of juggling, working in the evenings and weekends, emailing off essays to some crusty academic in Nuneaton, laboriously struggling towards the day when the fresh, re-trained you can be launched into the employment stratosphere. And when that day comes and you find a new job in a new field for the new you, you will go in at the lowest end of the salary, as Mrs Newie Newby, fresh out of college, with a twenty-four-year-old boss. Which can smart a bit when you're forty-one. Still, the fact does remain: you could always re-train.

RICE CAKES

Negative calorific value, but your child's main snack item until he is old enough to say 'biscuit'.

RIGHT . . .

Put this at the start of any sentence and you are signalling to your child that they are in big trouble, and signalling to yourself that you need to think of some quite creative punishment, right now. Right?

RISK

Flicking through a Mothercare catalogue when pregnant, you may have scoffed at the enormous range of safety kit available, from hob guards to furniture straps. What kind of an uptight, paranoid parent buys this shit? you wondered. Ha ha ha, the squares. I will never do that. My child will be free to explore its environment. How else is it to learn?

How indeed. After it's fallen off your coffee table for the sixth time, you realise that before children reach a certain level of maturity they do not learn. They just keep hurting themselves, with the average house providing a myriad opportunities for hurting to happen. Stairs, lamp flexes, artily placed vases filled with fresh flowers, staplers, the cat bowl . . . You are not being paranoid. This stuff is dangerous to kids. Furthermore, kids are drawn to danger like extreme-sports enthusiasts to a wet rock face. Time to take action. Time to make your home safe; to nail bookcases to walls, tape rugs to the floor, cover everything in bubble wrap and hermetically seal the windows. It's like you're expecting a bus-load of psychiatric patients to turn up. Or a hurricane.

This is being a responsible parent, isn't it? Well, up to a point. The problem with childproofing is that you can start to see danger where danger does not exist. Once your parental protective instinct kicks in, you can convince yourself that a cushion poses a grave threat to your infant's wellbeing. As for that pencil. It could get stuck in her ear. It could spontaneously fly off that table and spear her in the eye. Throw it out. Throw them all out. And those Biros. Potential death traps, every one.

As your child's world expands beyond your home the risks alter. Out there, it's a veritable Cambodian minefield of risk. Anything from an uneven pavement to a speeding 4x4 presents risk and you are powerless against all of it. This is why, when out with children, you are in a permanent state of alert. Code amber, if you like. Not exactly stressed, but not exactly relaxed, either. You learn to silence the voices that say 'we're doomed, doomed I tell you' as soon as you leave the front door, but they are always there threatening to pipe up.

You are doing the right thing, though, since exposure to risk is key to a child's development. If you keep him in, you risk him staring at hours of sub-standard telly or playing dodgy video games all day. Plus, when he does eventually go out he will be so incapable of assessing risk for himself that he will instantly get run over by a juggernaut. So you resist the urge to wrap him in cotton wool and lock him in the living room, and you let him explore the world. You let him climb that tree. If he falls, he will know not to climb it again. Something for him to reflect on while he's stuck in hospital for five weeks with both legs in traction.

Bingo! Right there is the problem with risk – it's risky. Even when the risk is small, its very existence suggests that the thing that just might possibly happen is *really* bad. When your child crosses a road, there is a risk that she will be hit by a car. Fine, it's a small risk, but you can't get hit by a car well. So to you it is a truly terrifying risk, irrespective of the odds of it happening.

Perhaps we need to be more like our parents, who were much less risk aware. They didn't go for poofy, precious stuff like stair-gates and car seats. They embraced a world where the only surfaces beneath climbing frames were concrete, where smoked-glass coffee tables were there to be smashed right through and cheap, additive-filled squash was available on tap.

Or maybe they were just negligent, and which would you rather be? Paranoid or negligent? It's a tough call, but I think paranoia wins. Just. So, if you don't mind, I'm off to check the batteries on my carbon-monoxide alarm. I could do it later, but I might forget, and that's a risk I'm not prepared to take.

ROUTINE

We just can't help it. Human nature seeks to create order and pattern out of the chaos of life. Even hippies are squares. Your pre-baby self might have been a laid-back, bohemian sort, but you will still have gravitated to a routine. You may have thought you were a fun-loving free spirit who liked to recklessly take your watch off and hang out at festivals, pogoing in your wellies and not brushing your hair, but come the working week, you probably still had muesli with half a chopped banana at 7.45 a.m. every morning and sat in the top-left fourth row from the front on the bus.

It's no surprise then that when the most chaotic event of your life happens, you desperately look to regain some semblance of control. Your baby is born and, after the first week of delighted cooing and impromptu popping in and out of cafés with your partner carrying an adorable newborn in a sling, you're left on your own, and it's bugger the cuteness, actually I'd like a shower (possibly every day?), I want a sandwich (maybe even at lunch time?) and I need four hours unbroken sleep (dare I suggest, at night?). You want time. You yearn for predictability. You crave *routine*.

But whose routine? Well, obviously you'd like your own. But getting a baby to fit in with your routine requires nerves of steel and some mind-bogglingly itinerised childcare manuals. It might involve you setting your alarm to drink a pint of water at 6.42 a.m. and blowing on your baby's feet to keep him awake outside of designated nap times. You might be advised not to look your wayward offspring in the eye when feeding at night in case you give him any crafty ideas that waking up at 3 a.m. could actually be fun. You'll have to sprint home with the buggy from your ante-natal group coffee morning in case your baby falls asleep before you've made it back to bundle him into his cot and slam down those blackout blinds by 11.59. Yes, regime might be a more pertinent term; perfect if you have a Swiss timepiece and the iron fist of a newly promoted sergeant major. Not so great if your watch broke two years ago and you just can't be arsed.

If you prefer your let-down reflex to be triggered by your baby crying rather than your mobile phone alarm, you might opt to adapt to your baby's routine instead. That'll go a bit like this. Get up way too early. Miss breakfast due to changing baby. Miss shower due to feeding baby. Go to baby music and pay £4.50 to sit in corner with sleeping baby. Miss lunch due to feeding baby. Go to supermarket. Abandon shopping basket in aspirational toiletries aisle. Take crying baby home. Feed baby. Despair as baby falls asleep one hour before bedtime. Bathe grumpy waking baby. Feed grumpy baby. Feed sleepy baby. Finally put baby to bed. Feed grumpy self. Go to bed. Get up to feed crying baby. Cry. Repeat daily.

Most of us hit upon a compromise between laissez-faire and super strict. We try to respond to our babies' needs whilst keeping to some sort of routine that involves fairly regular naps and mealtimes. This liberates us just enough to have an hour off roughly around 12.30 each day, which is pretty good after the round-the-clock chaos of life with a newborn. With a tiny bit of structure we gradually begin to make sense of the daunting world of parenthood. We become more confident and our growing kids thrive. Oh boy, do they thrive – on routine. At the age of four, they insist on thriving on it every time you pass the newsagent where you once bought them a Sherbert Dib Dab.

But beware, once routine has liberated you from the tyranny of unpredictability, it imprisons you in the daily grind. You become enslaved to your routine because, whisper it, it works. Don't tamper with it, for God's sake. Don't get fancy ideas about doing anything spontaneous or who knows what might happen. Ah, spontaneity. What happened to spontaneity?

Spontaneously combusted, that's what, the minute you signed up for parenthood.

RULE-BENDING

By dads. He knows how to do it right, he just can't be bothered.

By grandparents. 'Oh, Mummy doesn't like you having jelly babies at bedtime? Well, this will just have to be our little secret then.' Oh Grandad, you're so cool, aren't you, you interfering old tosspot.

S s

SCARE STORIES

Did you know that if your baby's socks are too tight they can stunt their growth?

SCHOOL

Your child starting school is a rite of passage. It's an emotional first snipping at the apron strings and, while it's exciting, deep down in the depths of your soul you feel uneasy. It's not that you would consider home educating your children, or that you are precious about letting them go, it's just that starting school is not so much them becoming part of a community, more you handing them over to The Man.

   Schools are constructed around rules, which are The Man's favourite thing. Some are reasonable, like 'we don't punch each other in the face': but others seem to be less about instilling a moral code, more about crowd control. My son's teacher slow hand claps as soon as the children become noisy. The kids then join in until they are all standing in a trance-like state, clapping rhythmically, and very much not chatting. How impressive! How scary! Another teacher has a rule that if it's getting too noisy you have to put your hand up. One hand going up prompts a Mexican wave of hand-upping, until all are up and silence reigns. I know, I know, when there are only two adults in charge of thirty kids you need strategies for keeping things tidy, but this is also how the few controls the many. This is how cults operate, with idiosyncratic rules and a sprinkling of brainwashing. These pliable young minds can be directed any old how. The teacher could just as easily tell them that if it gets too noisy they must stand on the desk and do a Nazi salute. (I'm glad she hasn't, though.)

Then there is the whole mystery of what they actually do, in there, all day. If you're lucky, your child may let fall a few nuggets: we had golden time (whatever *that* is), we did PE. If you're really lucky they may even dob on their classmates and tell you who had to sit on the 'thinking chair'. But otherwise, forget the casual informality of nursery, where you can wander in and chat with your child's carers daily. At school, your name's not on the door and you're not coming in. You are simply the courier service, delivering them to a room you rarely go into yourself, from which they emerge six hours later, with some pen on their clothes and perhaps a sticker, but otherwise, who knows? It's like the Mini Masons.

If ignorance is not bliss, the only option is to go under-cover – volunteer to help out in class. Those parents who volunteer do so not because they are altruistic, or because they really dig kids, but because they are just *dying* to see what goes on in there. They are stealth spying. While the other parents jostle and peep as the classroom door is opened a crack to admit their children, like onlookers at a crime scene, parents who volunteer to help are vetted by MI5, given a special secur-ity pass to flash at the teacher and are allowed under the police protection cordon and in. Once back on the other side, they are mobbed by those non-volunteering parents like a pack of red-top journos, braying for any gory titbits about what happened, who said what, to whom and what was the motive.

So. What do we know about school life? Very little. What we hope is that school will inspire, excite, stimulate. But what with Key Stages, national curricula and a whole testing regime governed by the need to produce league tables and hold schools to account, rather than help kids progress and think freely, you begin to fear that school is just a big sausage-squidger-outer machine producing identikit chipo-lata children adept in 'skills' that can be measured by society. Or maybe that's just me.

Oh and don't get me started on the whole knotty issue of whether children in Britain start school too soon. Compulsory education begins at five in England, Scotland and Wales, so that can mean children who have just turned four having to wipe their own bums and sit still in assembly. Now that *is* an education. Why can't we follow the Scandinavian example and just calm down about education? In Sweden, Denmark and Finland, school doesn't begin until the age of seven. Those lucky Scandie kids also get huge summer holidays – ten weeks in Sweden – whereas holidays in England and Wales are shorter than anywhere else in the European Union. They do better than us in European league tables, too. Finnish pupils start formal education at seven, enjoy eleven-week summer holidays and achieve the highest educational standards in Europe. If it works for Finland, why not here? That's the country that, let us not forget, produced The Moomins and Mika Hakkinen. I rest my case.

SEX

Each week a reader's problem is answered by three experts. This week: Help! I don't want sex.

Since I had my first baby six months ago I absolutely really don't want to have sex with my husband at all. He still desperately wants it and keeps attempting to make it happen by rubbing up against me in the kitchen (it's a narrow galley) and by buying 15 per cent Australian Shiraz, but after an exhausting day holding a baby I don't want to hold anything else in the evening. Is it OK not to have sex again (apart from, of course, at Christmas and when trying for another baby)? I need to know so I can tell him with confidence.

The post-menopausal big-bosomed bumptious national treasure agony aunt:
Dear me, lovey, you are in a pickle. Now, look, we've all experienced times where we just don't want a penis in our vagina, when it seems like a ghastly idea and we think, 'Oh bother, must I? I'd rather make some scones.' But sex is natural. Your husband has needs, and if you deny him them he will just get crosser and crosser. Even if you haven't had sex for donkey's years and don't feel like romping about starkers, you have absolutely got to get back in the saddle in order to maintain your relationship. My advice is to talk to him about how you feel, of course, but then to take the bull by the horns. Try starting with some light frottage (perhaps in your galley kitchen?) and build up to full-blown hanky-panky over a few nights. Grab life with both hands. Grab your husband with both hands! I'm sure you'll have a jolly time getting back on speaking terms with John Thomas. And he'll be happy! You'll know because he'll whistle at breakfast. He might even hang out the washing, too.

The sex therapist:
Sex operates on a use it or lose it basis, so you should attempt to have intercourse soon. Why not find a babysitter who can look after your child so you and your husband can spend the afternoon making love, or set the alarm early so you can make time for him before the baby wakes up? Try fondling, caressing or genital stimulation

first before allowing full penetration. Breathe. Relax. You might not experience full orgasmic response right away, but keep practising. Book the babysitter for at least another three sessions. With a small financial investment and a moderate level of effort, you will soon be back to optimal sexual functioning.

The mum of three:
Of course it is all right not to have sex! It's what got you into this mess in the first place, so no wonder your body is telling you never to do it again. Take a leaf out of my book. Wear a pair of very large pyjamas and retreat to the spare room. He'll soon get the message.

SHIT – GIVING ONE

It is quite hard to care. The stuff they get upset over. Oh come on, kids, stop being so, well, childish. So you didn't want me to break the biscuit in half? Whatever. Oh Christ, I've not gone and put the raisins in the wrong coloured bowl, have I? How can I ever apologise? You wanted me to squirt the soap onto your left hand, not your right hand. I've done it wrong again. Wrong! But you know what? IT DOES NOT MATTER! Right? I know you're only two, but it really, REALLY does not matter. In the scheme of things, you know, when you look at it on a larger, much larger scale, whether I cut up the fish-cake or you cut up the fishcake, *probably* – and I can't be 100 per cent sure – but probably will have very little bearing on the overall future of, you know, the world. And I'm quite tired. So I'm cutting up the fishcake. Then, when you cry, I'm going to go and sit in the other room for a bit. Might have a cry, too. We'll see.

SHOCK

At my (all girls') school we were taught a wide range of incredibly useful life skills, including conjugating Russian verbs, playing lacrosse, and origami. But not, unfortunately, child-rearing. Babies were only mentioned on a strictly biological and contraceptive need-to-know basis. We all recollect blushingly sharpening our 2H pencils to connect a diagrammatical vas deferens to an epididymis in a nicely rounded scrotum, and being forced at the age of eleven to watch some horrific slasher movie in the hall which turned out to be a late seventies representation of childbirth. Later on came the fondly remembered *wrestling the condom onto the test-tube* lesson. Ah yes. Those were the days. Looking back, it all seems to be a bit of a blur of blood and guts, cross-sectional pencil drawings and not-so-subliminal messages that only really quite mature ladies and bearded men who are married and love each other very much have babies. As far as my school was concerned, they were educating a generation of materials scientists, not mothers. They were so keen to dissuade us from fulfilling our biological role *prematurely*, it was never really acknowledged that the majority of us would go on to do it *at all*.

So we all (bar a couple of girls who were obviously bunking

off shagging on The Day of the Test-tube), left school without giving motherhood another thought. We merrily went our separate ways into various careers or low-paid but creative jobs and got on with the serious business of being independent, earning money and enjoying ourselves. So far so good.

Years later, I am thirty-two, noticing a few crow's feet, gradually losing my fashion sense and find myself dating a strange man with a strange beard. The not-so-subliminal messages return subliminally in my dreams. This is obviously it. He must be *the one*. All my thoughts seem to have become *italicised*. We fall in love. We get married. We throw all test-tube contraceptive caution to the wind. A child is born.

Now, for God's sake, pass me the smelling salts. As I gradually peel myself off the floor, I wonder what has hit me. Well, Motherhood, obviously. But why has it knocked me for six? I'm a woman after all, biologically predisposed for this moment. Yet I feel that dipping into a Miriam Stoppard and sniggering at the sieve in the birthing pool during a video in an NCT class has not been sufficient preparation. And it's not just the obvious inexperience, the lack of support networks or having to come to terms with the abrupt end of fifteen years of pleasing myself. It's bigger than that. It's culture shock writ large. The betrayal of a generation of women brought up in an era of second-wave feminism. WHY DIDN'T ANYONE WARN US???!!! What was the point of bringing us up to believe we could be like men? That we could achieve anything we wanted, have any job we liked? No one pointed out the elephant in the room that would fifteen years later trample all over our hard-won equality. No one suggested while pushing CLIPS leaflets on corporate law into our sixteen-year-old palms that this job would be great for making money, but impossible to do part time. No one ever advised us that we would need to earn at least 35k to make it affordable to return to work and provide childcare for two pre-school children. No one even explained that we might have to slightly under-use our Masters degrees in Economics to do a bit of admin at the local college if we intended to be around for the school run and summer holidays. Having instilled in us the belief, no, certainty, that we were equal to men, why weren't we warned that this right would expire when child-rearing began? One thing is certain. Until the (predominantly male) government enforces flexible working legislation and men, as well as women, decide to make use of it, our choices will never be equal.

It's a shocker all right. We've been hoodwinked and the advances of feminism have gone awry. You might as well ditch that B.Sc. in Biochemistry in favour of an NVQ in sock washing. Or if you're really advanced, perhaps you could try the Dip.Jug (*see also* Juggling).

SLEEP DEPRIVATION

'Blessings on him who invented sleep, the mantle that covers all human thoughts, the food that satisfies hunger, the drink that slakes thirst, the fire that warms cold, the cold that moderates heat, the common currency that buys all things, the balance and weight that equalises the shepherd and the king, the simpleton and the sage . . .' *Don Quixote*, part 2, chapter 68, Cervantes.

Yes, OK, OK, there's no need to go on about it, Don. We get the picture. Sleep is A. GOOD. THING. In fact, the greatest thing since, and before, sliced bread. Let's big it up for sleep, everybody. Yeah. Sleep. Woooh.

Well, you *would* if you were getting any. But unfortunately, you're not. You've experienced sleep deprivation before, of course. As a student, cramming desperately for exams, fuelled only by Pro Plus and chocolate biscuits. It felt fairly bad, even then. You remember the acne, the embarrassing involuntary eye twitching, the paranoia, the irritability, the blurred vision. Luckily it only lasted for two weeks and then you were free to sleep pretty much permanently for the next three months, rousing from your slumber periodically of an evening to stick a stamp on a job application and go to the pub.

This time it's serious. As a new parent you begin to understand why sleep deprivation has been used as the torture of choice by some of history's leading lights in unethical interrogation practices: Pinochet, the Japanese in the Second World War, the KGB, the South African government during Apartheid, ooh yes, and zooming straight in at No 1, the US Government at Guantanamo Bay. After a month with a colicky newborn you too are ready to admit to having attended terrorist training camps in Pakistan (honestly, loads of them!) if only someone will let you have four hours' uninterrupted shut-eye. As it stands, you've been having early starts, late finishes and numerous interruptions in between. Every night.

And you're suffering. The list of the physiological effects of sleep deprivation on Wikipedia reads like the small print on the back of a giant bottle of paracetamol that's been blended with arsenic and laced with malaria:

> Aching muscles, blurred vision, clinical depression, colourblindness, daytime drowsiness, loss of appetite, decreased mental activity and concentration, depersonalisation/derealisation, weakened immune system, dizziness, dark circles under the eyes, fainting, general confusion, hallucinations (visual and auditory), hand tremors, headaches, hyperactivity, hypertension, impatience, irritability, nausea, nystagmus, psychosis-like symptoms, sleep paralysis (while awake), pallor, constipation, slowed reaction time, slurred and/or nonsensical speech, sore throat, stuffy nose, weight loss or gain, severe yawning, decreased desire for sexual activity, delirium, death (in rats, but still . . .)

It's scary stuff, and not something you'd wish on your own worst enemy. You feel you can just about cope with the excessive yawning. You don't even mind the dark circles under your eyes (nothing a hint of concealer can't fix), and a bit of weight loss from your muffin top can only be described as a boon. But frankly, you're not really enjoying the tremors, the psychosis and the hallucinations. You may have gained a beautiful new baby, but you now appear to be losing your mind. Are you even human any more? You're not quite sure at 3.22 a.m. You wonder, in between feeding, tearing out your hair and slapping your palm repeatedly on your forehead, how the human race has continued for so long. How do parents look after babies when the very process of looking after babies turns parents into gibbering, malfunctioning wrecks?

Well, it doesn't last, as they say. One day, after a maddeningly inspecific amount of time (anything from two months to two years, just to keep you guessing) your baby will 'sleep through'. Once again you will be able to enjoy decent, uninterrupted periods of slumber (but only after you've got over the shock and stopped listening at their door every few hours for breathing). But don't get out the Champagne just yet. What with teething, illnesses, bad dreams and 6 a.m. singing sessions from your glad-to-be-alive eighteen month-old, you'll be yawning excessively for some time to come.

SNIFFING BABIES' ARSES

It's to see if they've filled their nappy. Women actually do this in public. Are there not easier ways of finding out?

SNOT

The taps turn on in late September and stay flowing until mid April. Get some tissues in.

SOCKS

Did you know that if your baby's socks are too tight they can stunt their growth?

SOFT-PLAY PLACES

Before you have kids you have no idea that such places exist. They are padded hangars on out-of-town industrial estates with no natural light and an aroma of nappies, where you pay several quid to squeeze yourself through tiny gaps on the top level of absurdly labyrinthine playing structures because your small child has got stuck. And the coffee's shit.

SPONTANEITY

Ooh, hang on, let me just check my family activity wall planner.

STUCK

Kids get stuck all the time. That's so daft. I rarely get stuck as an adult. I once got stuck in a lift – not my fault – and got a high heel stuck in a manhole cover, but that's nothing really. But kids. All the time. Stuck. They get stuck up poles and in swings and at the top of slides in the playground. Public spaces, while they may look fairly free of obstacles and tight corners, are a treasure trove of sticking opportunities to the under fives. Behind beach huts, under a stack of chairs, inside a roll of carpet (when shopping for carpet). You're no safer at home. They wriggle under the bed then can't get out. They clamber into your wardrobe then can't get out. They climb into their baby sister's cot then can't get out. Things get stuck on them, too – and not just stickers. Beans and peppercorns in ears, jars on fists, jumpers and potty seats on heads. Oh just stop it, will you? Shouldn't children be fitted with whiskers?

SUDDEN DEPARTURES, SLOW ARRIVALS

They want to go, go, go and you're suddenly out the door at 8.30 a.m. without having brushed your teeth. Then you take several hours to dawdle to your destination, like everyone is walking through cake mix.

SLOW ARRIVALS, SUDDEN DEPARTURES

Getting out of the door can take so very long, what with dressing, bag-packing, final wees. Then you get to your restaurant and have to order the bill with the food because once they've eaten a mouthful of main course and ripped up their napkin they've lost interest and it's, ACHTUNG! ACHTUNG! EVERYBODY OUT NOW!

SWIMMING

Ooh lovely. A thirty-length work-out of body and de-cluttering of mind followed by a cappuccino and a leisurely read of the papers. At least it is for those lucky child-free buggers in the big pool. For you it's forty-five minutes awkwardly squatting in 3 foot of slightly too cold water being periodically poked in the eye with a tube float. Followed by an expensive trip to the vending machine.

T t

TANTRUMS

The passionate self-expression of a frustrated infant, attempting to impose control upon an adult-centric and essentially chaotic universe? Or just bloody embarrassing when you're in Waitrose?

Well, a bit of both, usually. When they're not happening, you can understand why they do. Your child feels tired, frustrated, thwarted and, unable to pour himself a large drink, has a tantrum instead. Fine. But when they are happening, Christ alive, all that understanding runs for cover as you are rapidly swallowed up by an excruciating blend of embarrassment, rage and utter confusion.

It's a tantrum cliché that children stamp their feet, fling themselves to the floor and pound their fists like extras in an am-dram performance of The Crucible, but it's a cliché for a reason. They actually do it! If you have the misfortune to be in public when this happens, then added to your personal misery and alarm is the woe of feeling that everybody is watching. Which they are, because a child in full tantrum is a compelling sight. The chutzpah! The conviction! The complete lack of self-consciousness!

Of course, everyone is also watching *you*, to see how you deal with this fascinating predicament. Your child has thrown down the tantrum gauntlet, and you must take it up, but do you do it in a patient, sympathetic way or in a wrestling him off the premises way? That's a tough one. No one really knows how to deal with tantrums. Obviously, you should stay calm, but dealing with a red-faced, frothing three-year-old whose only concern is his own warped, infantile sense of justice and who has more energy than the National Grid when it comes to expressing his discontent is provocation of the highest order. Part of you may feel sorry for him as he spins into orbit, but another part will probably think, Dear God, child, would you ever just get a *grip*, you freakily emotional drama queen lunatic exhibitionist?

During the tantrum years, which, by the way, stretch far either side of the Terrible Twos – there's the Freakin' Threes and the Effin' Fours to contend with, too – every day can become a delicate tiptoe across a thousand eggshells. Anything can set them off, from car seat straps to the wrong sort of wind. It's like your child has turned into a hideous blend of Mariah Carey and Pol Pot: terrifying, dangerous and capricious. It can get to you.

You may, consequently, become a prisoner to your child's unpredictability, choosing to avoid any potential 'hot spots', which leaves you only your home or unpopulated areas with predominantly soft surfaces, like fields, to hang out in. But if you are brave and prepared to cock a snook at the dis-approving general public, you can carry on as normal, walk into that café with your head held high, asserting your right to be there, even though you know your over-tired child could blow at any moment and you're secretly bricking it that he will. Hell, you just want to enjoy a quick coffee in your local child-friendly café, but no café is *that* child friendly, so as your son begins the rapid descent into mini madness – THE BLACK! THE BLACK! – you hurriedly pack up, your latte still steaming, keeping your voice low but firm as you drag your rabid child behind you, the eyes of every punter in the place upon you. And all because he was given the wrong shaped biscuit.

If you can divorce yourself enough from the situation and placidly accept that you have now become the local pariah, you will see that tantrums are a truly spectacular phenom-enon. Like a volcanic eruption or a massive avalanche, they are awe-inspiring and raw. They're also really bonkers. If an adult did that, in public, because of a biscuit – no question about it, they'd be sectioned. But in a way, don't you wish you *could* do that? When life deals you yet another cruddy hand, don't you wish you could just fling yourself to the ground and writhe uncontrollably, screaming and turning puce, instead of having to weigh it up in your mind, moan a bit to your mates and ultimately put a brave face on it? Tantrums are just so much more honest, and honesty is good. Isn't it?

TEETHING

A catch-all term used to not-very-cunningly disguise our utter parental cluelessness.

While doctors fall over themselves to diagnose non-specific viruses, parents love to diagnose a spot of non-specific teething. Snot, diarrhoea, high temperatures, earache and sometimes even the appearance of the odd tooth are all blamed on it. My child must have about thirty-eight huge bastard pointy sharp molars. How about yours?

TELEVISION

We all know the statistics, and they are fairly damning. Too much television for young children has been shown to increase violent and aggressive behaviour, impair school performance, increase the risk of obesity and attention deficit disorder, and impede language development. A research paper by Cornell University in 2006 even suggested that sustained early exposure to TV could trigger autism. Similarly adverse affects could be achieved by pouring Coke onto their breakfast cereal, but that's not something many of us do regularly. So why are we all (happily or unhappily) letting our children watch so much telly?

Before your child is born you are convinced you won't

expose its innocent and impressionable young mind to the manifest evils of the box. That changes by about, ooh, day six, when you are sat on the sofa breast-feeding and relying on *Diagnosis Murder* to alleviate the tedium. This feels just about acceptable. Your baby is staring at your boob, not at Dick and Barry Van Dycke, after all. If he can't see more than two feet in front of him, antiques programmes and afternoon American crime dramas are not going to pervert his tiny mind.

Then it comes to weaning. You find the spoon goes in a lot more easily when your baby is busy staring at flickering images over your shoulder. But it's just distraction, isn't it? A troupe of cartwheeling chimps would have the same effect, but won't really fit into your dining room. The TV will have to do. It's OK, though – he's not *watching* it, just *looking* at it. There's a difference. You hope. And if it means he unwittingly eats five ice-cubes of puréed Cabbage Surprise, then it's staying on.

Then comes the decisive turning point. He starts to crawl. Great, another milestone ticked off. But shit! How do you *stop* him moving? He makes a bee-line for the oven and rugby tackles the rubber plant. How can you *function* when all this suicidal mayhem is going on around you? Sixties mums opted for the playpen. Caging toddlers was the only way they got a bit of housework done. For our generation, with twenty-four-hour multiple-channel programming, however, TV is the new restraining device. When you need to scrub the kitchen floor or take a shower without him emptying your purse into the goldfish bowl in your absence, *In the Night Garden* will do nicely. And it's so much more humane. Look! No bars! He is free to move whenever he chooses. But you know he won't. He is rooted to the spot, in a trance, with his mouth slightly agape, a line of dribble oozing down his chin.

So you admit it. He *does* watch television now. But you make sure it's the *right* sort of television. No one ever turned into a 23-stone illiterate axe-murderer from watching the *Fimbles*, did they? Yeah – and this TV lark could even be educational. Pop on a Baby Einstein and he's practically tripping out in spasms of subliminally ingested intelligence. Well, either that or he's fitting. No, it's not so bad. CBeebies only and lengthy post-programme discussions about gender stereotyping in *Thomas the Tank Engine*. It's all well under control.

Then he starts school. He's tired and overwrought at the end of his first day. You let him relax in front of the box and foolishly decide that a bit of classic *Tom & Jerry* on Cartoon Network would be worthwhile viewing. A serious error. Before you know it, his after-school telly-watching routine is set in stone. His emergent literacy and numeracy skills enable him to channel surf dementedly. CBeebies is for babies. He is now only interested in programmes with characters called Megablade and Knucklebuster, which you find a little discomfiting. And then there are the commercials. With the critical faculties of a peanut, he's bowled over by them all. You find him humming advertising jingles instead of nursery rhymes. Oh God, it's all gone horribly wrong. (*See also* Advertisements.)

Still, when a playdate goes pear-shaped or you fancy a lie-in on a Sunday morning, the terrible guilt is outweighed by a whopping great dollop of relief. Yes, on reflection, for overworked and overstretched parents, television is very definitely a *necessary* evil. Has any one seen the remote?

TODDLER GROUPS

Why do they exist? Good question. According to the commercialisation of babydom bandwagon-jumper-on-ers, they are a fun way to stimulate your baby. Whether it's singing, signing, tumbling or yoga, they're going to 'improve' your baby. Really bring her on. Because she's been slacking off a bit in her first year, and it's about time she pulled her socks up, no?

For you, though, they are just something to do that isn't wandering around your local shopping centre eyeing up things you can no longer afford or shadowing your baby as she delightedly climbs up the stairs for the twenty-seventh time while you try to half listen to a play about antiques dealers on Radio 4.

So you pick up some flier from the library showing beaming babies having a right royal knees-up and decide that Tiny Tiddles Rootlin' and Tootlin' Time is the answer. And let's not be too cynical, here. At first look, it may seem like the answer. As you take your place in the circle of mums and babies, you think, How enchanting: all these cutey bubsies sitting on a carpet chewing maracas, while everybody sings jolly songs. Happy mums' faces glowing as they bounce their little ones on their knees, simulating donkey rides. Space for your crawling child to explore. Fun, education, stimulation, company. Maybe even a custard cream at the end. What's not to like? So you sign up for a course of six. Every Tuesday at 2 p.m. you'll be down the local church hall, without fail. It will get you both out of the house and, especially now it's winter, what better way to fill an afternoon?

Ah, but there are better ways. There *must* be better ways.

Next week, the scales fall from your eyes like a thousand tiny tambourines crashing to the floor. Any fantasies of making chummy new mum mates quickly evaporate as you notice how a smug mum music group faction already exists. They've been coming for weeks and know *all* the words to 'Go To Sleep Bonnie Baby'. Do *you*? Pah! Amateur. Nothing for it but to hover about on the margins, taking an extra long time getting baby's coat off and unpacking snacks from the buggy to distract yourself from the fact that you're being ignored. The other kids are a crack squad of elite instrument grabbers, too, always first off their mums' laps when the musical bits and bobs are tipped onto the rug, ready to elbow any less ruthless nine-month-old out of the way as they swipe the really swanky cymbals, leaving only a dribble-encrusted kazoo and a broken click-clacker for your less ballsy, but now very disappointed infant.

Once the fun starts, you might notice fewer warm smiles and more cold draught blowing across the dusty floor. Your baby's schedule may have slightly changed in the last week, too, so instead of being bright-eyed and attentive, this week, he's asleep for the first ten minutes, awake but breast-feeding for the next and only ready to grapple his jingle bells for the final song. You notice the woman who leads the group has a bloody awful singing voice, not a mellifluous purr as you'd originally thought, and isn't a warm earth mother, but a failed actress in her fifties who smokes fags outside the hall and doesn't really like babies, not having had any herself.

So you wonder why you're here. Some of the babies are getting restless. Some are beginning to cry. One has bashed another over the head with a frog castanet. A couple of toddlers have legged it across the hall to play peek-a-boo behind the stacked chairs. Anarchy is breaking out. But there's no opportunity to mull all this over because up you get, it's time to march around the room in a circle, singing. Only listen. The babies aren't singing. No. Because they can't. It's just you, and a group of other women in their mid thirties, who you don't know from Adam. Rootlin'. And then tootlin'.

TOMATO KETCHUP

So much more than just a condiment, ketchup is the elixir of a three-year-old's life. Run out at your peril.

TO WORK OR NOT TO WORK?

Well, there you were, pre children, most likely either doggedly plodding or dynamically powering along in your full-time job, getting paid a salary, holidays, sick pay, a nice company pension scheme, a ready-made social life and free doughnuts on a Friday to boot. Up until then you hadn't really noticed any appreciable gender inequality in the workplace. Well, now you come to mention it, only one or two on your board of executives wore a bra, in the office anyway, but *you'd* always found it fairly easy to find gainful employment and you were promoted ahead of that knob Martin, after all. Just before you got carried away acting like you were permanently living in an episode of *This Life*, however, all that changed. One day, you peed on a stick and, hey presto, your working life was never the same again:

Day 1 – Phewbloomingwhee! Very relieved to find that company at least has adequate maternity benefits. Was so much more interested in the foreign travel and discounted gym membership perks when took job six years ago. Kicking self that didn't accept extraordinarily dull job in British Council when had chance, though. Twenty-six weeks on full pay, thirteen weeks on statutory maternity pay, thirteen weeks on no pay and the right to request a five-year career break somehow make it look a lot less fuddy-duddy public sectorish now. Always wondered why that Jiig Cal career profile matching thing at school suggested Assistant Prison Governor or English Teacher for all the girls who had been thinking perhaps corporate law or TV production might suit. Perhaps trying to tell us something? Should possibly have taken note.

One year later – Gorgeous baby born and life turned upside down. First few months gone in whirl of magical highs, desperate lows, poo, milk, poo and sleep deprivation. Just about getting hang of having no real friends and being able to do impromptu nappy changes in town without having a nervous breakdown. Then, more shit. Old boss has called asking about return to work. Work! Had forgotten all about that, so far removed is it from dribble and pelvic floor exercises. What to do?

One year one day later – In turmoil of confusion. If go back to work full time, bohemian earth mother cousin will smile patronisingly then tell mates am hard-nosed materialist bitch who had no business having child if didn't intend to look after her. If stay at home full time, friends in office might think am dull-witted bovine sap who spends days make-up-less and in comfortable shoes, wallowing in brain-mulching drudgery and watching *Loose Women*. God, have lost count of number of times have been asked what actually do all day and baby is only six months old. Mother-in-Law's face already suggests she thinks am busy spending precious son's hard-earned cash on over-priced lattes and Cath Kidston tea-cosies instead of cleaning house son is currently generously paying large mortgage on.

One year two days later – Epiphany. Realise doesn't matter what other people think. Should follow heart – go with what I think. Shit. What *do* I think? Have found adjusting to motherhood v hard but am almost loving it now. Baby being delightful. Enjoying feeding ducks every day and quite getting into watching Hollyoaks while doing evening feed (me that is, though baby seems quite happy also). Feel baby needs me. Would miss her dreadfully. But need money. And also miss sociability, intellectual stimulation, financial independence and status of working life and do not want to jeopardise career progression after sixteen years' education and twelve years' hard sodding slog.

One year three days later – Epiphany. Realise want to work part time. In my dreams, would have same pay, status and career prospects as had before and excellent company crèche for precious child.

One year ten days later – Epiphany. Realise am living in cloud-cuckoo-land. Work has politely considered part-time working request as per Government legislation and generously offered a two-month period of four-day working, then returning to five days as job can't be done effectively part time for spurious 'business' reasons. There is no crèche. Suggest partner might consider requesting part-time or flexible work if am possibly having to resume full time. Partner spits out coffee. Think this means no.

One year eleven days later – Realise can either work full time and feel guilty about potentially (according to all sorts of reports whirling round exploding brain) damaging childcare, stay at home full time and worry about lack of money and long-term job prospects, or get a different part-time job. Look up part-time jobs. Consider monumental lack of personal experience and motivation in cleaning, catering and cashiering industries and pittance of pay in relation to childcare costs. Resolve to stay at home for time being and attempt to set up hand-painted eco cake-cases business whilst baby naps and whilst fantasising about living in Copenhagen.

Two years later – Second child born. No chance of going back to work now – even full time. Childcare for two under three will cost 20k and only used to earn 22k after tax anyway. Fledgling cake-case business also goes to wall when discover that children won't obligingly sleep/play independently during working hours.

Six years later – Second child has started school! Think about returning to work full time. Call up old company to test waters. Human Resources director says, off record, that am about as useful to him now as chocolate teapot, or indeed, a newly qualified college leaver, only college leaver will request precisely zero days off for looking after sick children and attending nativity plays. Note that Martin the office knob is now Marketing Director and that wouldn't want to work for him anyway.

Six years one day later – Think about 're-training' in job that would fit well round school hours and holidays as partner now on stratospheric career path that means working twelve-hour days and only taking two weeks' annual holiday. Resolve to call the Prison Service and the British Council straight away.

TRASHING

Kids trash houses. Even nice kids do.

They are drawn to buttons and dials and switches like we are drawn to red wine and Kettle Chips. A toy mobile phone is just that. A *real* mobile? Now you're talking. It has lights and numbers and, if you're really lucky, someone will speak to you through it. Maybe an alien? Ace!

All but the most anal parents can make their home child-friendly – that's to say, rammed with enough toys to distract the young ones from the white goods and the furniture – but take them to a real adult's home, one where children rarely enter, and you will see how poorly children fit into a grown-up, first-world environment.

When playing in the garden of their grandparents' immaculate home your child will repeatedly kick the football into the pretty, groomed flowerbeds. Shit! Mind the peonies! He will dredge the pond for mini beasts using a large stick. Shit! Mind the goldfish! He will bat shuttlecocks up into the guttering. Shit! Mind the guttering! Oh, actually, don't worry

about that one . . . Back inside, he will want to explore your
father-in-law's recliner chair. Of course he will. It has buttons.
It moves. It's like some kind of Power Ranger Megazord driving
seat, for Christ's sake, and you're asking him not to touch it.
Are you crazy?

This is not wilful trashing, though. It's youthful explor-
ation, exuberance and curiosity, which are good things. Minds
are being fed here, experience garnered, sofa cushions crushed
to buggery and previously clean paintwork marked by a
hundred greasy handprints.

It's not really their fault. Like domesticated animals, we
have removed children from the wild and forced them to live
within our adult-centric environment. Consequently they pee
on our rugs and leave muddy footprints all over the floor,
much as a cat or dog might, because they don't quite suit a
grown-up's world, with its emphasis on cleanliness and 'nice
stuff'.

Of course, in the old days it was far more acceptable to be
a child. When you live in an iron-age hut and your children
spend most of their time outside, there is so much less for
them to trash. And consequently, so much less for you to hassle
them about. What are you going to say? 'Get out of that
midden, will you, it's filthy.' 'Don't play with that torc, it's
the only bit of jewellery I've got.'

So kids into the modern domestic environment won't go.
It's called the trashing equation. Easy to learn, applied every
day.

TREATS

What they are:

1. Assuagers of guilt. You don't need to spell out to your child that the hot chocolate he is enjoying was purchased to make you feel better about being withdrawn and snappy all day, but it was and it might.
2. A positive way to give in. You do not have the strength to say no to your child's bleating for an ice-cream. No problem, just call it a treat and you can kid yourself that you are happily indulging her, not pathetically caving in.

What they are not:

1. Doggy chocs.

TRYING TO READ THE PAPERS

We all do it. Silly old us. We've seen it on the telly. It looks so nice – kids playing on the carpet while their parents sip coffee and read the papers on a weekend morning. Ha ha ha ha ha. FORGET ABOUT IT! Kids have a sixth sense for any signs of adults pursuing their own interests. The merest rustle of a broadsheet will set their antennae twitching. They cannot abide you reading the papers. It's forbidden. Put it down.

Reading the papers becomes a huge bargaining tool between

Mum and Dad, too. Just as map-reading is a classic car-based row, who gets to read the papers is the subject of many a weekend flare-up. Dads will often try to do it surreptitiously. They've gone into the kitchen to make junior a piece of toast and before you know it they're stuck into the Comment section. Women go for a more all-out emotional appeal. They will say, 'Could I just have ten minutes reading the paper?' What they're actually implying is, '. . . which is nothing really, after I've put my life on hold and my body through turmoil to bring up your children, and all I want is a paltry ten minutes with the colour supplement, so don't even contemplate denying me this.'

But who are you trying to kid? It's just a paper, not a fundamental human right. It's a handful of interviews and some overpriced handbags, not your ticket to intellectual nirvana. You know you'll just look at the pictures and read the captions, anyway.

T-SHIRTS WITH SLOGANS ON

Just as clothing manufacturers have decided, in their infinite wisdom, to turn a blind eye to the sexual revolution and create predominantly camouflage-print clothes for boys and sickly pink clothes for girls, they have also hit upon the idea of the humorous slogan T-shirt.

Some of these we have made up, some, sadly, are available at all good retailers . . .

My Rules, My Way
Your Life in My Hands
All Daddy Wanted Was a Blowjob
Spank Me
Lock Up Your Daughters
Too Cool To Drool
Cute as a Bastard
My Mummy is a Yummy Mummy
My Daddy is a Motherfucker
I Shit Liquid
I Wish I'd Been Born a Girl
I Am the Ressurrection and the Light
Stand Well Back – I Puke
I Want Always Gets
I Bloody Love Tantrums, Me
Insomniac Hyper Space Mutant Fuckwit

U u

UMBRELLA

After having a child, an umbrella is about as useful to you as a pair of crotchless panties. It's not that it won't be raining or that the experience of birth has awakened a primal urge in you to be at one with the elements. More that you have confronted the physical impossibility of steering a buggy one-handed. Now you realise why all mums wear anoraks. They're not total squares, they just need a hood. You attempt to go down that route, too. You swallow your fashion sense and embrace your inner train-spotter. You soon discover, however, that a hood is fine for walking in straight lines, but useless when it comes to going round corners or crossing roads. Turn your head to the left and your hood remains resolutely stationary. Was that an articulated lorry coming towards you or just a bit of blue Gortex flapping in the wind? Better not take any chances. Keep the hood down and both hands on the buggy. Embrace the wet look, and invest in some waterproof mascara.

UNDERAPPRECIATED – often

UNDERFUNDED – routinely

UNDERWEAR – grey

USURPED

As soon as you have a child you both know that you love it more than you now love each other. It's like when Diana was talking about Camilla. 'Yes, there were three of us in our marriage, umm, rather crowded, yes.'

V v

VACCINATIONS

It's not easy for babies. You're only two months into life outside the womb, can't even burp on your own, and someone starts sticking needles into you. Big, sharp ones. Into your teeny thigh.

At the vaccination clinic the waiting room is rammed with babies, looking happy or indifferent or asleep, and parents, looking unhappy or riddled with guilt and fear. You are so disturbingly aware of what's coming. He's so blissfully *not*. If you're early, you get to work yourself up into a further state of anxiety as you witness the interminable vaccination process. The nurse calls cheerfully for the next baby, the door shuts, there's a pause of about three minutes during which time chat in the waiting room becomes palpably strained, then a baby's cry pierces the atmosphere. The mums exchange nervous glances.

When it's your turn, you'll clamp your baby into your lap, expose his flawless skin and try not to catch his eye as he beams up at you, enjoying his little outing as the lady in blue does something in his peripheral vision, then wham – stabs him in the leg. And again, on the other side! Jesus! Most babies are too shocked to cry at first. Their tiny brains take a few seconds to catch up with what just happened. 'We were having such a nice time, Mummy, I don't understand . . .' Are you imagining it or do they look up at you with a face that says. 'How could you?' And before they let out that howl, aren't their tiny baby lips just forming the word 'Judas'?

VACILLATION

The Calippo or the Feast? The Feast? Yes? No? The Calippo then? For God's sake, hurry up! The freezer's open! I'm counting to three. One, two, two and a half . . .

Small children and decision-making don't mix. Offer them anything more than a choice of one and their heads explode. They can't help it, their critical faculties aren't sufficiently developed to enable them to evaluate information and make proper decisions. They lack both knowledge and experience, which leads to irritating daily incidents of prolonged vacillation. Will it be the pink skirt or the lilac one? Obviously it'll be the pink. Or maybe the lilac. No pink. Definitely pink. Unless it's the lilac.

They're not just being contrary little buggers, of course. They do try to weigh up their options. It's just that the criteria

they use are a bit *unsophisticated* for making many of the decisions they are faced with. 'Is it the biggest?' isn't a bad frame
of reference for selecting an ice-cream. Somewhat less effective for choosing, say, which pair of socks to wear in the
morning. So unless you have a spare few years to spend simply
grinding your teeth, just hang-fire on offering those decision-
making opportunities. When you insist on him having
porridge and wearing his wellies to school, rest assured that
far from being authoritarian, you are actually sparing him a
brain-frazzling ten minutes of pointless deliberation.

And sparing yourself an expensive trip to the dentist.

VAN

You used to have a cool VW Beetle. Now you have a car that
looks suspiciously like a van and three car seats.

VENTING

Uncle Quentin had it easy. When those pesky Famous Five
children made him angry, he could shut himself in his study
for the weekend, bellow really loudly at them, or call his disappointing daughter George a jolly stupid idiot. He only had to
display a spot of genuine hair-ruffling affection towards them
once every hols when the plucky kids had outwitted some
nasty men with revolvers or solved a serious crime.

But that was 1942. Anger management for today's morally-
restrained parents is a bit more of a challenge. We aren't

allowed to lose our rags or disappear for 48 hours. We have to bottle up our fury and carry on. This would be disastrous for our blood pressure if it weren't for the development of specialised techniques for managing the *strictly controlled venting of suppressed rage*. Forget counting to 10 and grinding your teeth, these are the most effective ways of letting off (a tiny bit of) steam:

Whispering child-directed expletives and insults
In the face of a persistently annoying child being persistently annoying, the positive parent of today smiles and suggests a spot of Moonsand sculpting whilst murmuring 'iwishyou wouldjustfuckoff' slightly under her breath.

Growling – the new shouting
Today's reasonable parent identifies that yell emerging from her diaphragm, and then skillfully contains it in her throat, mouth closed, rolling it into a short bear-like growl. This can sound a little odd, obviously, but has the added benefit of limiting the amount of bad swear words released into the childhood environment.

Doodling – going mad with a pad
When your child volubly declines to eat her home-made shepherds pie, manically scribbling a series of Munch style faces screaming 'HELPME!!!!' can prove quite cathartic.

Just remember to put the evidence in the shredder afterwards.

VIOLENCE

Like the opening scene from 2001: *A Space Odyssey* – where the ape picks up a bone and immediately begins smashing things up with it – small boys in possession of a stick will not fashion it into a water diviner or whittle it into a charming walking cane, they will attempt to twat their friends over the head with it. They can transform any long straight item into a sword and just about anything at all into a gun, whether it be a bent paper clip or a fishfinger. They will then use it to fire at your head. Often first thing in the morning.

You can agonise over nature versus nurture and fill your home with non-gender-specific toys, but I'm going to stick my neck out here and suggest that nature will always win, hands down. She wants little boys to be full to the brim with testosterone and ready for action at all times. That's why a playful tickle can speedily turn into a wrestling bout and a tots' disco can suddenly resemble Altamont. One minute they're gambolling round like playful lambs, the next they're scissor-kicking each other or punching themselves in the head to get a laugh.

As well as re-enacting violence, little boys like to watch it. The news will do, as there's something unutterably compelling about a tank or a rifle or a ruddy great helicopter gunship to a four-year-old. 'Is that a gun?' my son will shriek, bouncing up and down on the sofa, scarcely able to believe his viewing luck, as some grim story about Afghanistan unfolds.

When it comes to TV drama, their checklist of requirements

is simple. Explosions = good. Napalm = super top. Martial arts moves = excellent. If a young boy could direct his own film it would look like a cross between *Apocalypse Now* and *Crouching Tiger*, with a giant cigar-smoking Pingu as the lead, tooled up like he's a member of the Lord's Resistance Army, indiscriminately taking out Daleks. Perhaps.

It's no wonder that kids are drawn to violence, not repulsed by it. The version pitched to them is pleasantly benign. When the Power Rangers get zapped by an evil alien, they make a slightly annoyed 'huuurgh' sound, like someone has just crept up from behind and given them the Heimlich manoeuvre. Then they triumph and say 'yeah' a lot. And do some high fives. Yeah!

There's no alternative, mind you. You can't expose them to the reality of violence. They tried that back in the seventies with a raft of public information films aimed at primary school kids, highlighting the dangers of pretty much everything. One focused on the violent consequences of playing on a railway line. The resultant carnage on a group of innocent eight-year-olds once the 12.10 to Waterloo had powered through was gruesomely portrayed. Most of the juvenile audience to this 'drama' just threw up and cried. Talk about driving your point home. What was wrong with the bloody Green Cross Code man, anyway? Not Tarantino enough?

VOMIT

Just tell yourself it smells like Parmesan cheese.

V SOUNDING LIKE B

Many kids mix up their letter sounds when making their first forays into communicating. One of the classic casualties is the letter V, which can end up sounding like B. Most of them grow out of this habit, but some individuals carry it into adult life. Examples are peppered throughout popular culture. There are the great pop songs, including 'He Ain't Hebby, He's My Brother' by The Hollies and 'Temptation' by Hebben Sebbenteen. Hardy wrote *Tess of the D'Urberbilles*, but his publishers forced him to change the title and Martin Luther King's famous speech of 1963 actually began 'I hab a dream' (but they edited that on the tapes).

W w

WEANING

Your baby is several months old. At long last, whatever your feeding choice, you've got the milk business sussed. If you opted for the breast, your nipples will have toughened up admirably under sustained abuse, like a pair of ten-year-old boarders starting their spring term at Eton. If you went with the bottle, you can now make up six in under two minutes whilst watching GMTV and cooking a full English. Just when you're feeling confident enough to get out either breast or bottle in public without having to seek absolution from the local Catholic priest, however, a new set of feeding issues arrives and beats you vigorously about the head with a plastic spoon. To wean, or not to wean? Now *that* is the question. Do it at four months and you're (suddenly) contravening Government, nay World Health Organisation, advice. Wait till six months and your mother will be overcome by paroxysms of rage and righteous indignation. After all, she weaned you onto Farley's Rusks and a tin of Carnation at eight weeks and it never did *you* any harm. Early or late, whenever you start, it's a thrilling milestone. How exciting! What could be more natural and instinctive than providing grub(s) for your very own baby bird? Surely it's a mere logistical exercise; a simple dialogue between a captive infant and a plastic spoon?

Well, of course it's not. Your child may be captive in the sense that he's imprisoned in his Stokke TrippTrapp, but his attention is shot. Mentally he's sitting in the dog basket taking his clothes off and gleefully waving a rubber bone. He cares not a jot for itinerised mealtimes, and will lean, duck, wriggle and spit like a loose hosepipe in order to prevent you from getting a spoon anywhere near him. And the amount of paraphernalia required to feed a person with a stomach the size of a conker is, quite frankly, mind blowing. You're looking at a microwave, a high chair, a low chair, a blender, numerous plastic spoons, bowls, plates, bibs, several ice-cube trays, assorted Tupperware pots, jars, tins and pouches. Not to mention the manuals and recipe books. You will probably need at least two Annabel Karmels and a Gina Ford in order to perfect Twelve Ways with a Pulverised Sweet Potato. And whatever challenging concoctions you may devotedly purée and freeze, or tempting organic roasted root vegetable compotes you may buy, you find that they all look the same. And that same is, well, vile. There's something about reducing a roast dinner to the consistency of porridge and then popping a lid on it that makes it seem a lot less like roast dinner, and a lot more like wallpaper paste.

It's understandable, then, if parents feel they are all puréed out and become a little twitchy at the sight of moulded plastic feeding implements. Maybe it's time to think outside the blender and try a different approach. That is, *baby-led* weaning. A genius time- and money-saving idea in which you don't wean your baby with spoons. He handily weans himself, without. Bin the blender and cast out the cutlery. This approach somewhat controversially calls a solid a solid and not a smoothied three-bean and spring vegetable cassoulet. Instead of rudely assaulting your baby's delicate mouth and unsuspecting palate with various flavours of slurry, simply let him forage for scraps from your dinner plate. Thenceforth, every mealtime, let him 'share' platters of carrot sticks, lightly steamed broccoli and lumps of banana with you, gradually varying the types and texture of foods. By seemingly guiding his own consumption from the off in this way, your child should develop an admirably healthy attitude to food. Five years down the line, you'll find him independently tucking into a moderate-sized portion of steak tartare with a watercress salad on the side. It sure beats dry toast and a Frube.

Ultimately, however you tackle the weaning process, don't beat yourself up about it. Whatever you do, by the age of three, he'll be super keen on sausages, but highly suspicious of spinach. And they'll all, most definitely, scream for ice-scream.

WHAT'S HOT

The essential style barometer for today's trendy tots and their parents:

Naming your children after fruit/Old Testament figures/fifties tradesmen We're thinking Pomegranate, Absalom and Reg. Too cool!

Knitted swimming costumes Very retro-conscious. Your kids will be itchy, but oh so chic

Trainer bras for four-year-olds As seen at Karl's recent Miami show

Bread and dripping Our new downfall. We know we shouldn't, but we can't resist that meaty, fatty fix

Giving kids coffee For the buzz of Sunny D, the natural way, it *cannot* be beaten

Stickers We've said it before, we'll say it again, badges are o-u-t, OUT!

Slapped cheek The models at Prada's Milan show all sported the flushed-face look – very now

Hot Wheels The 2009 collection is just in. Could we *be* any more excited?

Hot milk Served in a plastic beaker at bedtime. Beyond fabulous

Hot housing Do you want your kids to grow up thick? Duh, no!

Fart jokes OMG! *Sooo* funny

Poppers Totally working for us. Way quicker than buttons, way more fun

Nappies for women Genius idea! Perfect for busy mums on the go

The Wottingers The cool family *du jour* – never knowingly overexposed

WHAT'S NOT

Knitted socks A vintage revival too far. See also mittens on string

Slippers Like, beyond winter 2008. Proper indoors children know it's all about cashmere socks this year

Spelling Did we mention we thought it was overrated? C'mon, people, what's your spell check for anyway?

Bedtimes Overexposure = us finally realising how boring they are

Thumb-sucking Even knowing that Stella McCartney does it cannot win us over. Umm, sorry, no

Cellular blankets Quite possibly the most unwarm blankets ever invented

The Pontipines Have we not mentioned them before? Hasten ye to the CBeebies website to learn more of their frankly implausible chimney-jumping stunts

Pa Pontipine's tache We're getting the eighties eebie-geebies just thinking about it – *trop* Burt Reynolds in *The Cannonball Run*

WHINGEING

In parents: I never get to do the things I want to do.

In kids: I never get to do the things I want to do. And I want more juice.

WHY QUESTIONS

When you first have kids, you fondly imagine a time when your baby will be a toddler and will badger you with all those probing 'why' questions. You lovingly picture the sweetly intense enquiries of a blossoming mind, trying to discover more about the world.

The reality is, of course, somewhat different. Your child will not in fact be asking why the toast fell off the table downwards and not upwards or sideways, or why Mummy, does a benevolent God let war and famine occur? Whatever you may think of her precocious talents, she currently has the intellectual capacity of a demented chimp. (Yes, they can also blow kisses on demand and wee in a potty for a chocolate button.) The why questions are not, at this point anyway, the sign of burgeoning genius. They are merely the child's first inept forays into conversational language. Not so hot on the old witty repartee at this early stage, she will say 'why?' to most opening and subsequent conversational gambits. She is capable of saying it seven times in under thirty seconds. And it is fist-clenchingly annoying. You will scare yourself by morphing into your mother – spitting 'Because it just is!', 'Because I said so!', and 'What did I just say?' through gritted teeth.

So what to do?

As that venerable old sage Gary Barlow once advised, just have a little patience. Earplugs are also most effective. (Well, they are, although he didn't say that.)

WIPES

Baby wipes have taken over the world. As seemingly essential to mothers as rice cakes and patience, they are a sinister menace because:

1. They are impostors! Masquerading as innocently damp tissues, they have chemically more in common with a Brillo Pad. Plastic, polyester, cellulose and cleaning fluid make for a startlingly unbiodegradable bit of kit. They'll still be floating their way across to Hawaii by the time your child has grandchildren.

2. They seem to have scarily industrial cleaning properties. Pen on the wall? Sudocrem on the carpet? Motor oil on your hands? Forget Vanish and Swarfega. A baby wipe will do the trick. Come to think of it, maybe they could dissolve cellulite, too?

3. They are unbelievably strong. You'll never succeed in breaking one, should you decide you only need half a wipe. In fact, if you tied a whole pack's worth together, you could quite possibly bungee jump safely out of your bedroom window. Impressed with their

evident durability, my son even suggested we sew some together to make a jacket.

4. They have brainwashing capabilities. Baby wipes have caused modern mums to lose the ability to remember how they might have cleaned bums and faces on the move before their invention. Flannel rubbing, cotton wool dabbing and spittle thumbing are all (rightly or wrongly) dying arts.

5. They are always *on offer*. Two for the price of one. If you have ever bought a full-price pack of wipes you must have been mad or desperate. Because they are always half price it is hard to resist buying such a useful bargain. Either those manufacturers are lovely and generous to new mums or the wipes are actually only worth half the money in the first place. Hmmm.

6. They multiply. You go to pull one from the handy plastic packet dispenser thingy, and four more follow in hot pursuit. But it's OK. Why just use one when you can use five? Well, what the hell. They were on offer anyway . . .

WORLD SHRINKAGE

You daredevil, you've been to school and back twice *and* over to Sainsbury's today. Do you have jet lag?

Courtesy of your infant, your whole world is now a micro neighbourhood comprising school, shops, post office, park, supermarket, doctor's. It's like you are on a piece of elastic attached to your home. You do the school run then ping back, out to the park then ping back, round to the corner shop then ping back. You will walk the same routes each day, slowly. You will see the same faces and visit the same shops for the same items (milk, bread, Frubes, grapes). Life becomes very small. You can remain in your town for days, weeks, months even, without venturing beyond its parameters, and when you do, it is only to visit that farm park six miles away that you went to a few Sundays back. Or your mum's. There are now also places that you never visit at all: pubs in the early evening full of after-work drinkers, major cities, antiques shops, boutiques of any persuasion. Gone, quite gone. When you do venture out without children, further than the park or the school, you will feel giddy and strangely exposed, but also shocked at the price of public transport, like someone who has been out of the country for the last five years and is fresh off the plane. Which is quite a good analogy for life with young kids, when you think about.

WOTSITS

See also Quavers.

X x

X FACTOR

The X Factor is fantastically educational TV and we would recommend that all parents sit their children down to watch and learn.

They can see the age-old good cop, bad cop dynamic played out in glorious colour courtesy of Simon Cowell and Cheryl Cole. Cowell: 'Are you mad? Have you had a labotomy? Awful, quite awful.' Cole: 'You're just not quite right for us, pet.'

There are some basic lessons in singing, too. What is good and what is very, very bad (those twin sisters with NHS glasses who worked in an envelope factory in Clitheroe spring to mind).

X Factor also tests a child's emotional literacy. Is the contestant crying because she's happy or because she's sad? Did she get through? So why is she upset? You might also ponder together a few ethical questions, such as is it appropriate to offer up people who clearly have special educational needs as entertainment? Finally, your child will learn what an X looks like and how to make one with their arms, like all those gibbons queuing up for the auditions.

A quality evening's entertainment and educative, too. And so much better than a bedtime story.

X-RATED

Should you ever misguidedly wish to indulge in the act of copulation again once you have had a baby (*see also* Sex), you will have a few child-shaped obstacles to overcome first. You may have a heavy-breather snuffling away in a cot beside you with a prior and more urgent claim on your mammaries. You may have a miniature co-sleeper or two nightly starfishing across your bed. Even if you have successfully reclaimed your own room/bed/breasts, you may still feel the need to have your door wide open to listen out for crying/vomiting/breathing/absence of breathing coming from other bedrooms during the night. Considering you used to freak out if you caught so much as the cat lazily watching you doing it from the corner of its eye, there's no longer much hope for you in the hanky-panky stakes. Now it seems that all-comers are welcome to the 'marital' bed. You might as well get a webcam. Ah well, at least you can dispense with the pills and condoms. It's coitus interruptus all the way now. The thought of a small child rushing in to join the fun at 6 a.m. will probably be all the contraception you need.

XYLOPHONE

Or is it a glockenspiel? Every child has one, but few will ever go on to rival Sir Patrick Moore. Pity.

Y y

YELLING

In parents: any instruction to your kids will have a far more effective response if your neighbours can hear it, too.
In kids: well, wouldn't you if you were given carrot batons instead of discs?

YESTERDAY

'What, the day before this day?' Blimey, when do kids get a basic concept of time? Maybe the year after this one.

YOU BROUGHT IT ON YOURSELF – THAT ARGUMENT

Time and again, when women are bold enough to write about the negative sides of being a parent, some numpty will dish out the astonishingly stupid and short-sighted retort, 'You wanted to have kids, so it's your fault.' Similarly, for every individual who, on an online parenting forum, anonymously laments the exhaustion, despair and anxiety that many women experience with a baby or toddler, another will tell her, finger wagging accusingly, that she wanted to have kids, so stop moaning.

The pointlessness and lumpenness of this argument is so striking it hardly needs pointing out, but it's indicative of how harshly women who become mothers are judged. If someone has a car crash, you don't rail at them for driving in the first place. If someone takes on a job that involves computer work then develops RSI, you don't shrug and say, What did you expect? Many decisions in life involve risk and having kids is definitely one of those. It can be great, but it can also be a perfect pain in the parts. What's wrong with saying so?

There are a gazillion column inches given over to upper-crust nits recalling their gruelling trek from pole to pole wearing only hessian Speedos or some such, and countless sobby sob stories by D-list celebs piffling on about their addiction to Lemsip or whatever. They all brought that on themselves, but they get far less roundly criticised for it. So why do mums get shut up and put down? After all, being a mother only involves months of nausea, violent childbirth, chronic sleep deprivation, very sore boobs, loss of personal freedom, loss of career, loss of identity, wearing an anorak, watching the *Tweenies*, and overexposure to playgrounds, Play Doh and playdates . . . Oh, stop whining. Just get on with it, woman.

YOU'LL NEVER WALK ALONE

When you walk through a storm, hold your head up high . . .
and for God's sake don't forget the weather shield. Yes, from
now on you will be surgically attached to a buggy or sling
whenever you leave the house. You have morphed into a not
particularly comedic double act like Bob Carolgees and Spit
the Dog and will not perform on your own in public for a
good while yet. If you do manage to slip out of the house for
two minutes to buy a pint of milk while your mother holds
the baby, neighbours and shopkeepers will demand to know
where he is, as if you have somehow recklessly mislaid your
more important other half. Without the buggy, you will feel
naked and exposed. You may need to relearn your walk – the
insouciant stroll of the woman *sans* infant and its transporta-
tion device. You will also have to work out what to do with
your arms, which are currently metronoming madly at your
sides now that you have no handles to grip. Perhaps you could
casually tuck one hand into your pocket. Or take up smoking.

True, the sling is not so bad. It feels quite organic and
kangaroo like; akin to waddling around with your enormous
pregnancy bump, but a bit less likely to cause you to piss yourself in public. And if the baby's asleep and a bit on the small
side you can almost forget she's there – relaxing, yes, though
somewhat perilous when it comes to partaking of elevenses.
The buggy is a different matter, however. Feeling as though
you are wrestling a wayward office chair down the high street,
it's hard to get used to the fact that you have to take such an

unwieldy contraption out with you wherever you go. There can be no more opportune dashes across busy roads to catch the bus. In fact, no more devil-may-care bus catching at all. No more tripping gaily down staircases or sidling through narrow doorways, hopping over puddles or squeezing into busy shops. There are so many places that are inaccessible to you now, you begin to realise how wheelchair users are discriminated against. Faced with another huge flight of stairs, a lift out of order or two minutes to catch your train, all you can do is stand helplessly, tears welling, at the mercy of other people's goodwill. And they might help you or they might not, depending . . .

And this is how it'll be for the next three years. Just you and your buggy. Dependent on strangers, walking only in straight lines and on very flat surfaces.

YOUR PARTS

I don't know what to call them. And neither will you. Your lady regions. Your secret womanly places. Your chuff. Your muff. Down below. But anyway, it takes a beating. And not just during labour. During pregnancy, as the growing baby bears down upon your pubic girdle, you may feel like you're having a permanent prolapse, which is unpleasant and sometimes inconvenient. When you're bathing, your low-slung undercarriage can actually stick to the bottom of the bath, in the way that a suction pad on a car sun-shade sticks to a window. It can also hoover up an impressive two pints of bath water to be released some time later, often much later, and it takes you a week or two to work out that you're not, in fact, incontinent. They don't warn you about this in the manuals.

Your hair grows abundantly during pregnancy, which is fine on your head, but not on your chuff. And nature has the last laugh here because, due to your expanding bump, you won't even be able to monitor your wayward hairline. Immerse yourself in a bath and you can simulate footage of an underwater kelp forest, swaying in the current.

Time was that your fanny was a region associated with sex and intimacy. Once pregnant and certainly once in labour, it will have become the subject of so much interest that you may wish you'd had the foresight to install a turnstile and charge for access. A good midwife will be able to establish how dilated your cervix has become during labour by how many fingers she can insert in its neck. Not had a baby? Oh, you're wincing now, but you wait. When she can get a fist and a sovereign ring up there you'll be ecstatic. And by the time you've got the baby out, you won't care any more. They can stitch you, they can swab you, they can crochet your pubes into a tea cosy. Hell, they can video your nethers and stick them on YouTube for all you care. Just no more childbirth for you, please. At least, not today, anyway.

Z z

ZEE OR ZED

Now he knows his ABC, he can sing along with me.
But only if he's prepared to say zee.
If he says zed, he'll have more street cred –
But a really, rubbish rhyme.

ZERO TOLERANCE – VIA DAD

He's come in from work, he's feeling macho, he's not standing
for any nonsense, but he's also not that articulate, so try to
suppress a smile when he uses sub-Victorian-dad language in
an attempt to discipline his child. Things like, 'Now perish
the thought that this sort of behaviour continues. You know?
Hmm? If it does I shall be really just so extremely cross. I mean,
for Pete's sake. It behoves you to do better, frankly, it really

does, and I want you to have a jolly good think about how you've made us feel, which is very sad. And when I come back in, *when* I come back in here, this room, yes? If you still haven't tidied up, OK, then I mean, it's like, *woe betide you.* And if you're NOT VERY CAREFUL, I WILL HAVE TO SHOUT AT YOU!'

ZUT ALORS!

Yes, *Zut Alors!*, as our French friends might exclaim. Or Holy Blooming Mackerel! From conception to birth to starting school, what a journey it's been. We've experienced tears, laughter, poo, more tears, happiness, a smattering of wretchedness, £3,000 worth of coffee and cake, and plenty of chilly afternoons in the playground.

Before you jumped on the parenting bandwagon, your emotions seemed to be on a fairly even keel. You were very happy that day in 2002 when you got promoted, of course, and really quite distraught when the dog died. But on a daily basis, your feelings usually jogged gently along. It was business as usual – you knew pretty much what to expect. But not any more. Now you're a parent you feel as though you're doing the emotional equivalent of a triathlon. Every day. Before breakfast.

Within the grinding predictability of a day with small children (up at six, trip to the park, lunch, cake, tea at five, bath time, bedtime, *Property Ladder*, repeat . . .) lurks a world of emotional surprises. You can experience the ecstatic highs of gazing on your sleeping baby, just after the desperate loneliness

of a 4 a.m. feed; the life-affirming joy of bouncing on a trampo-
line and chasing pigeons with a two-year-old, a mere half an
hour before the fear and loathing of a full-blown tantrum. You
can feel happy and loving and fulfilled and frustrated and bored
and miserable, all in one routine-filled, groundhog day of
parenting. You can cope with the lows, because amidst all
the mayhem, your child may suddenly stroke your face, or
amusingly ask you for some new Pimps for PE, or spontaneously
tell you in the voice of the most charming, tiny munchkin that
they will love you for ever and ever. And so you go on.

And time goes by. Before you know it, your tiny dot is a
budding, fairly well-balanced four-year-old and off to school.
Even if you're not quite sure how you made it here, take a
moment to reflect. You've survived your child's first, most
dependent years. And so has she. Have a break. Take five. Crack
open the custard creams. You can breathe a sigh of relief. Well,
for now, anyway.

Apparently teenagers are an effing nightmare, but therein
lies another tale . . .

ACKNOWLEDGEMENTS

We would like to thank the Random House team, especially Rosemary Davidson, Sue Amaradivakara in Publicity, Claire Morrison and Claire Wilshaw in Marketing, Simon Rhodes in Production, Greg Heinimann in Design, and Christina Usher and the whole sales team, for all their hard work and enthusiastic support. Thanks also to Chris Hemming and Steve Lowe, for casting critical eyes over many early (and late) drafts, and for all-round encouragement of the endeavour; to Tristan Jones for a supportive reading of the proposal, and to Cathy Whitelock and Sarah Pocklington for reading early drafts and providing vital feedback and enthusiasm. Thanks to our Mums for going through it all with us 35 years ago, and above all to our beautiful children and all their lovely little friends for providing so much inspiration – without them, this book would not have been possible.